PALAU AND THE COMPACT OF FREE ASSOCIATION WITH THE UNITED STATES

AMERICAN POLITICAL, ECONOMIC, AND SECURITY ISSUES

Additional books in this series can be found on Nova's website
under the Series tab.

Additional E-books in this series can be found on Nova's website
under the E-books tab.

PALAU AND THE COMPACT OF FREE ASSOCIATION WITH THE UNITED STATES

JAMIE-LYNN BERKIN

AND

PATRICK D. O'SHAUNESSY

EDITORS

Nova Science Publishers, Inc.

New York

For permission to use material from this book please contact us:
Telephone 631-231-7269; Fax 631-231-8175
Web Site: http://www.novapublishers.com

NOTICE TO THE READER

The Publisher has taken reasonable care in the preparation of this book, but makes no expressed or implied warranty of any kind and assumes no responsibility for any errors or omissions. No liability is assumed for incidental or consequential damages in connection with or arising out of information contained in this book. The Publisher shall not be liable for any special, consequential, or exemplary damages resulting, in whole or in part, from the readers' use of, or reliance upon, this material. Any parts of this book based on government reports are so indicated and copyright is claimed for those parts to the extent applicable to compilations of such works.

Independent verification should be sought for any data, advice or recommendations contained in this book. In addition, no responsibility is assumed by the publisher for any injury and/or damage to persons or property arising from any methods, products, instructions, ideas or otherwise contained in this publication.

This publication is designed to provide accurate and authoritative information with regard to the subject matter covered herein. It is sold with the clear understanding that the Publisher is not engaged in rendering legal or any other professional services. If legal or any other expert assistance is required, the services of a competent person should be sought. FROM A DECLARATION OF PARTICIPANTS JOINTLY ADOPTED BY A COMMITTEE OF THE AMERICAN BAR ASSOCIATION AND A COMMITTEE OF PUBLISHERS.

Additional color graphics may be available in the e-book version of this book.

Library of Congress Cataloging-in-Publication Data

Palau and the Compact of Free Association with the United States / editors, Jamie-Lynn Berkin and Patrick D. O'Shaunessy.
　　p. cm.
　Includes index.
　ISBN 978-1-62100-064-8 (hardcover)
　1. Palau--Foreign relations--United States. 2. United States--Foreign relations--Palau. 3. Economic assistance, American--Palau. 4. Technical assistance, American--Palau. I. Berkin, Jamie-Lynn. II. O'Shaunessy, Patrick D.
　JZ2050.A57U6 2011
　327.966--dc23
　　　　　　　　　2011030128

Published by Nova Science Publishers, Inc. + New York

CONTENTS

Preface   **vii**

Chapter 1   Compact of Free Association: Proposed U.S. Assistance
to Palau and its Likely Impact   **1**
United States Government Accountability Office

Chapter 2   Statement of H. E. Johnson Toribiong, President of the
Freely Associated State of Palau   **23**
H. E. Johnson Toribiong

Chapter 3   Testimony of Frankie Reed, Deputy Assistant Secretary
of State, Bureau of East Asian and Pacific Affairs,
"Compact of Free Association with the Republic of
Palau: Assessing the 15-Year Review" ·   **31**
Frankie Reed

Chapter 4   Statement of Anthony M. Babauta, Assistant Secretary
of the Interior-Insular Areas, Department of the Interior,
"The Agreement between the Government of the United
States of America and the Government of the Republic
of Palau following the Compact of Free Association,
Section 432 Review"   **39**
Anthony M. Babauta

Chapter 5   Testimony of Robert Scher, Deputy Assistant Secretary
of Defense, South & Southeast Asia, "Department of
Defense's Support of the Palau Compact Agreement
Review"   **45**
Robert Scher

Chapter 6   Compact of Free Association: Palau's Use of and
               Accountability for U.S. Assistance and Prospects for
               Economic Self-Sufficiency   **51**
               United States Government Accountability Office

Chapter 7   Palau Profile   **141**
               United States Department of State

Chapter Sources   **147**

Index   **149**

PREFACE

The Compact of Free Association between the United States and the Republic of Palau, which entered into force in 1994, provided for several types of assistance aimed at promoting Palau's self-sufficiency and economic advancement. Included were 15 years of direct assistance to the Palau government; contributions to a trust fund meant to provide Palau $15 million each year from 2010 through 2044; construction of a road system, known as the Compact Road and federal services such as postal, weather and aviation. U.S. agencies also provided discretionary federal programs related to health, education and infrastructure. This book explores the provisions for economic assistance to Palau, its impact on the trust fund's likelihood of sustaining scheduled payments through 2044 and the projected role of U.S. assistance in Palau government revenues.

Chapter 1 - The Compact of Free Association between the United States and the Republic of Palau, which entered into force in 1994, provided for several types of assistance aimed at promoting Palau's self-sufficiency and economic advancement. Included were 15 years of direct assistance to the Palau government; contributions to a trust fund meant to provide Palau $15 million each year from 2010 through 2044; construction of a road system, known as the Compact Road; and federal services such as postal, weather, and aviation. U.S. agencies also provided discretionary federal programs related to health, education, and infrastructure. In 2008, GAO projected total assistance from 1994 though 2009 would exceed $852 million.

Chapter 2 – This is a testimony of H. E. Johnson Toribiong, President of the Freely Associated State of Palau, Before the Senate Committee on Energy and Natural Resources.

Chapter 3 - This is a testimony of Frankie Reed, Deputy Assistant Secretary of State, Bureau of East Asian and Pacific Affairs, Before the Senate Committee on Energy and Natural Resources.

Chapter 4 - This is a testimony of Anthony M. Babauta, Assistant Secretary of the Interior – Insular Areas, Department of the Interior, Before the Senate Committee on Energy and Natural Resources.

Chapter 5 - This is a testimony of Robert Scher, Deputy Assistant Secretary of Defense, South and Southeast Asia, Before the Senate Committee on Energy and Natural Resources.

Chapter 6 - The Compact of Free Association between the Republic of Palau and the United States entered into force on October 1, 1994, with the U.S. interest of promoting Palau's self-sufficiency and economic advancement. The compact and its related subsidiary agreements provide for a 15-year term of economic assistance. In fiscal year 2009, the two governments must review the terms of the compact and related agreements and agree on any modifications. The Department of the Interior (DOI) has primary responsibility for oversight of Palau's use of compact funds. GAO was requested to report on (1) the provision of compact and other U.S. assistance to Palau in fiscal years 1995-2009; (2) Palau's and U.S. agencies' efforts to provide accountability over Palau's use of federal funds in 1995-2006; and (3) Palau's prospects for achieving economic self-sufficiency. GAO reviewed Palau's compact annual reports, financial statements and internal control reports for fiscal years 1995-2006, as well as other compact-related documentation. GAO interviewed officials from the U.S. and Palau governments and conducted fieldwork in Palau.

Chapter 7 - Palau was initially settled more than 4,000 years ago, probably by migrants from what today is Indonesia. British traders became prominent visitors in the 18th century, followed by expanding Spanish influence in the 19th century. Following its defeat in the Spanish-American War, Spain sold Palau and most of the rest of the Caroline Islands to Germany in 1899. Control passed to Japan in 1914 and then to the United States under United Nations auspices in 1947 as part of the Trust Territory of the Pacific Islands.

In: Palau and the Compact of Free Association ...   ISBN: 978-1-62100-064-8
Editors: J. Berkin and P. D. O'Shaunessy   © 2012 Nova Science Publishers, Inc.

Chapter 1

COMPACT OF FREE ASSOCIATION: PROPOSED U.S. ASSISTANCE TO PALAU AND ITS LIKELY IMPACT

United States Government Accountability Office

WHY GAO DID THIS STUDY

The Compact of Free Association between the United States and the Republic of Palau, which entered into force in 1994, provided for several types of assistance aimed at promoting Palau's self-sufficiency and economic advancement. Included were 15 years of direct assistance to the Palau government; contributions to a trust fund meant to provide Palau $15 million each year from 2010 through 2044; construction of a road system, known as the Compact Road; and federal services such as postal, weather, and aviation. U.S. agencies also provided discretionary federal programs related to health, education, and infrastructure. In 2008, GAO projected total assistance from 1994 though 2009 would exceed $852 million.

In September 2010, the United States and Palau signed an agreement (the Agreement) that would, among other things, provide for additional assistance to Palau and modify its trust fund.

This statement describes (1) the Agreement's provisions for economic assistance to Palau, (2) its impact on the trust fund's likelihood of sustaining scheduled payments through 2044, and (3) the projected role of U.S. assistance in Palau government revenues. GAO reviewed the Agreement; examined Palau's recent single audit reports and budget projections; and assessed trust fund balances and disbursement plans under various assumptions and investment returns.

WHAT GAO FOUND

The Agreement would provide steadily decreasing assistance totaling approximately $215 million from 2011 through 2024 (see figure). This would include the following:

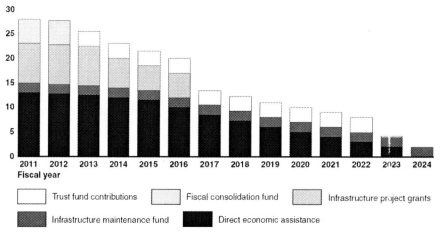

Source: GAO analysis of the Agreement between the Government of the United States of America and the Government of the Republic of Palau Following the Compact of Free Associa tion Section 432 Review.

Assistance to Palau Specified in the Agreement Dollars (in millions).

- direct economic assistance ($107.5 million) for government operations,
- infrastructure project grants ($40 million) to build mutually agreed projects,
- infrastructure maintenance fund ($28 million) for maintaining the Compact Road, Palau's primary airport, and certain other major U.S.-funded projects,
- fiscal consolidation fund ($10 million) to assist Palau in debt reduction, and
- trust fund contributions ($30.25 million) in addition to the $70 million contributed under the compact.

Under the Agreement, the United States would contribute to the trust fund from 2013 through 2023, and Palau would delay its withdrawals by $89 million from 2010 through 2023. GAO projects that with these changes the fund would have a 90 percent likelihood of sustaining payments through 2044, versus 25 percent without these changes.

Estimates prepared for the Palau government project declining reliance on U.S. assistance under the Agreement—from 28 percent of government revenue in 2011 to under 2 percent in 2024—and growing reliance on trust fund withdrawals and domestic revenues. The estimates show trust fund withdrawals rising from 5 percent to 24 percent, and domestic revenues rising from 40 to 59 percent, of total government revenue. According to the estimates, U.S. assistance from 2011 though 2024 would total $427 million, with discretionary federal programs accounting for about half of that amount.

Chairman Bingaman, Ranking Member Murkowski, and Members of the Committee:

I am pleased to be here today to discuss the September 2010 agreement between the U.S. and Palau governments.[1] The Compact of Free Association between the Government of the United States and the Government of the Republic of Palau, which entered into force in October 1994, provided for several types of assistance aimed at promoting Palau's economic advancement and eventual self-sufficiency.[2] In addition to establishing Palauan sovereignty and U.S.-Palau security and defense arrangements, the compact provided economic assistance to Palau.[3] This assistance comprised, among other things, direct economic assistance for 15 years to the Palau government; the establishment of a trust fund intended to provide Palau $15 million annually from 2010 through 2044; investments in infrastructure, including a major road; and the provision of federal services, such as postal, weather, and aviation. The compact also established a basis for U.S. agencies to provide discretionary federal programs related to health, education, and infrastructure. In June 2008, we projected that U.S. assistance to Palau from 1995 through 2009 would exceed $852 million, with assistance under the compact accounting for about 68 percent and assistance through discretionary programs accounting for about 31 percent.[4] We also reported, in 2008, that the likelihood of the Palau trust fund being able to sustain the planned payments through 2044 was uncertain.

The September 2010 agreement between the U.S. and Palau governments (the Agreement) followed a formal review of the compact's terms required 15 years after it entered into force.[5] Provisions of the Agreement would, among other things, extend economic assistance to Palau beyond the original 15 years and modify trust fund arrangements. A bill now pending before the U.S. Senate would approve the Agreement and appropriate funds to implement it.[6]

My statement today describes (1) the extension of economic assistance to Palau as outlined in the Agreement, (2) the impact that this assistance would have on the Palau trust fund's sustainability, and (3) the projected role of U.S. assistance in Palau government revenues.

For this statement, we reviewed the Agreement, assessed trust fund balances and disbursement plans under various assumptions and investment returns, and examined single audit reports and budget estimates prepared for the Palau government. We determined that these data were sufficiently reliable for the purposes of our review. We conducted our work from February to June 2011 in accordance with all sections of GAO's Quality Assurance Framework that are relevant to our objectives. The framework requires that we plan and perform the engagement to obtain sufficient and appropriate evidence to meet our stated objectives and to discuss any limitations in our work. We believe that the information and data obtained, and the analysis we conducted, provide a reasonable basis for any findings and conclusions.

BACKGROUND

Palau consists of 8 main islands and more than 250 smaller islands with a total land area of roughly 190 square miles, located approximately 500 miles southeast of the Philippines. About 20,000 people live in Palau, concentrated largely in one urban center around the city of Koror, and more than one-quarter of the population is non-Palauan.[7] Palau's economy is heavily dependent on its tourism sector and on foreign aid from the United States, Japan, and Taiwan.[8] Similar to many small island economies, Palau's public sector spending represents a significant percentage of its gross domestic product (GDP).[9]

U.S. relations with Palau began when American forces liberated the islands near the end of World War II. In 1947, the United Nations assigned the United States administering authority over the Trust Territory of the Pacific Islands, which included what are now the Federated States of Micronesia, the Republic of the Marshall Islands, the Commonwealth of the Northern Mariana Islands, and Palau. Palau adopted its own constitution in 1981. The governments of the United States and Palau concluded a Compact of Free Association in 1986; the compact entered into force on October 1, 1994. The Department of the Interior's (Interior) Office of Insular Affairs (OIA) has primary responsibility for monitoring and coordinating all U.S. assistance to Palau, and the Department of State (State) is responsible for government-to-government relations.

Table 1. Key Provisions of Palau Compact of Free Association and Subsidiary Agreements

Compact section	Description of key provisions
Title one: Government Relations	*Sovereignty* Established Palau as a self-governing nation with the capacity to conduct its own foreign affairs. *Immigration privileges* Provided Palauan citizens with certain immigration privileges, such as the rights to work and live in the United States indefinitely and to enter the United States without a visa or passport. This privilege remains in effect as long as the compact agreement is not amended by mutual agreement or mutually or unilaterally terminated.
Title two: Economic Relations	*Compact direct assistance* Established 15-year term of budgetary support for Palau, beginning on compact's effective date. This support included direct assistance for current account operations and maintenance and for specific needs such as energy production, capital improvement projects, health, and education. *Trust fund* Required the United States to contribute to a trust fund for Palau. *Compact Road* Required the United States to construct a road system (the Compact Road).[a] *Compact federal services* Required the United States to make available certain federal services and related programs to Palau, such as postal, weather, and aviation. The compact subsidiary agreement implementing such services was in force until Oct. 1, 2009.[b] *Accountability for compact funds* Required Palau to report on its use of compact funds and required the U.S. government, in consultation with Palau, to implement procedures for periodic audits of all grants and other assistance.
Title three: Security and Defense Relations	*U.S. authority for security and defense matters* Established that the United States has full authority and responsibility for security and defense matters in or relating to Palau, would take action to meet the danger of an attack on Palau, and may conduct activities on land, water, and airspace as necessary. *Strategic denial* Foreclosed Palau to the military of any nation except the United States, unless they are invited by the United States and under the control of the U. S. armed forces.

Table 1. (Continued)

Compact section	Description of key provisions
	U.S. defense sites and operating rights Established that the United States may establish land and sea defense sites in Palau and has certain military operating rights. The subsidiary agreement implementing this provision provides the United States exclusive use of certain land adjoining the airport and certain submerged land in Malakal Harbor and remains in effect through 2044. *Service in the armed forces* Established eligibility of Palau citizens to serve in the U.S. armed forces. The provisions on U.S. authority for security and defense matters, U.S. defense sites and operating rights, and service in the armed forces remain in effect unless the compact is terminated by mutual agreement or, if the compact is unilaterally terminated, until October 1, 2044, and thereafter as mutually agreed. The strategic denial provision remains in effect through 2044 and thereafter until terminated or otherwise amended by mutual consent.
Title four: General Provisions	Established general provisions regarding approval and effective date of the compact, conference and dispute resolution procedures, and compact termination procedures. Required reviews of its terms on the 15th, 30th, and 40th anniversaries of the compact's entry into force—that is, in 2009, 2024, and 2034, respectively.

Source: GAO analysis of the Compact of Free Association between the Government of the United States and the Government of the Republic of Palau.

Notes: The compact's subsidiary agreements relate to specific titles of the compact; in many cases, they contain implementing details of compact provisions.

[a] The compact called for the United States to build the Compact Road according to mutually agreed specifications before Oct. 1, 2000. The road was completed and turned over to Palau on Oct. 1, 2007. See GAO-08-732, Appendix V, for more information.

[b] *Federal Programs and Services Agreement Concluded Pursuant to Article II of Title Two and Section 232 of the Compact of Free Association*, which took effect in 1995, established the legal status of programs and related services, federal agencies, U.S. contractors, and personnel of U.S. agencies implementing both compact federal services and discretionary federal programs in Palau. Under this agreement, the United States Postal Service (USPS) conveys mail between the United States and Palau and offers other services such as Priority Mail®, Collect on Delivery (COD), and USPS Domestic Money Orders. Palau maintains its own postal service for internal mail delivery. Under this agreement, the National Weather Service (NWS) reimburses Palau for the cost of operating its weather station in Palau, which performs upper air observations twice daily and as requested for the purpose of Palau's airport operations and the tracking of cyclones that may impact other U.S. territories such as Guam; and the Federal Aviation Administration (FAA) provides aviation services to Palau, including en-route air traffic control from the mainland United States, flight inspection of airport navigation aids, and technical assistance and training.

Key provisions of the compact and its subsidiary agreements address the sovereignty of Palau, types and amounts of U.S. assistance, security and defense authorities, and periodic reviews of compact terms. Table 1 summarizes key provisions of the Palau compact and related subsidiary agreements.

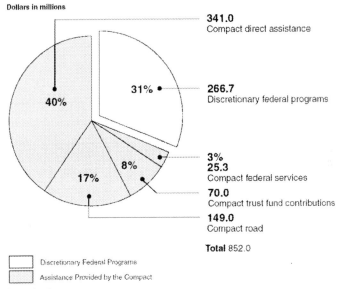

Dollars in millions

341.0
Compact direct assistance

31% **266.7**
Discretionary federal programs

40%

3%
25.3
Compact federal services

17% 8%

70.0
Compact trust fund contributions

149.0
Compact road

Total 852.0

☐ Discretionary Federal Programs
☐ Assistance Provided by the Compact

Source: GAO analysis.

Notes:

All years are fiscal (Oct. 1 – Sept. 30) and all dollar amounts are in current (i.e., nominal) dollars.

Numbers may not add to 100 percent due to rounding.

Amounts shown for compact direct assistance, compact trust fund contributions, and Compact Road are based on Interior's Office of Insular Affairs' actual and estimated payments to Palau for 1995-2009, as reported in its budget justification to Congress for 2009.

Amount shown for compact federal services is based on GAO estimates of past expenditures by the NWS, USPS, and the FAA.

Amount shown for estimated discretionary federal programs is the sum of (1) U.S. agency program expenditures as reported in single audits for 1995-2006 for the Palau national government and for 1997-2006 for the Palau Community Action Agency and the Palau Community College, (2) GAO estimates of U.S. agency program expenditures for 2007-2009, and (3) GAO estimates of DOD Civic Action Team costs for 1995-2009. Estimated and projected federal program expenditures do not include the value of U.S. loans to Palau. For more information, see GAO-08-732.

Figure 1. Projected U.S. Assistance Provided to Palau in 1995-2009.

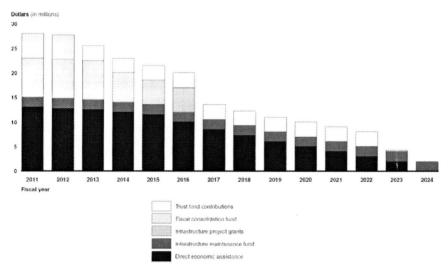

Source: GAO analysis of the Agreement between the Government of the United States of America and the Government of the Republic of Palau Following the Compact of Free Association Section 432 Review.

Note: Compact federal services and discretionary federal programs are not included in this analysis.

Figure 2. U.S. Assistance to Palau for 2011-2024, as Outlined in the Agreement.

In addition to the U.S. assistance provided under the compact, U.S. agencies—Education, Health and Human Services (HHS), and Interior, among others—provide discretionary federal programs in Palau as authorized by U.S. legislation[10] and with appropriations from Congress. (See app. II for a complete listing of these programs in Palau.)

In our 2008 report, we projected that from 1995 through 2009, U.S. assistance to Palau would exceed $852 million, with economic assistance provided under the compact accounting for 68 percent and discretionary federal programs accounting for 31 percent of this total (see figure 1).[11]

AGREEMENT WOULD EXTEND U.S. ASSISTANCE FOR 15 YEARS, DECREASING ANNUALLY

The September 2010 Agreement between the U.S. and Palau governments would extend assistance to Palau to 2024 but steadily reduce the annual amount provided. The Agreement would also extend the authority and framework for U.S.

agencies to continue compact federal services and discretionary federal programs.[12]

Assistance to Palau Would Decline through 2024

Key provisions of the Agreement would include, among others, extending direct economic assistance to Palau; providing for further investments in infrastructure; establishing a fiscal consolidation fund; and making changes to the trust fund. U.S. assistance to Palau under the Agreement would total approximately $215 million from 2011 through 2024.[13] The pending legislation would authorize and appropriate funds to Interior for this assistance.[14]

- *Direct economic assistance* ($107.5 million). The Agreement provides for direct assistance—budgetary support for government operations and specific needs such as administration of justice and public safety, health, and education—of $13 million in 2011, declining to $2 million by 2023. The Agreement also calls for the U.S. and Palau governments to establish a five-member Advisory Group to provide annual recommendations and timelines for economic, financial, and management reforms. The Advisory Group must report on Palau's progress in implementing these or other reforms, prior to annual U.S.-Palau economic consultations.[15] These consultations are to review Palau's progress in achieving reforms[16] such as improvements in fiscal management, reducing the public sector workforce and salaries, reducing government subsidization of utilities, and tax reform. If the U.S. government determines that Palau has not made significant progress in implementing meaningful reforms, direct assistance payments may be delayed until the U.S. government determines that Palau has made sufficient progress.
- *Infrastructure projects* ($40 million). The Agreement mandates U.S. infrastructure project grants to Palau for mutually agreed infrastructure projects—$8 million in 2011 through 2013, $6 million in 2014, and $5 million in both 2015 and 2016. The Agreement requires Palau to provide a detailed project budget and certified scope of work for any projects receiving these funds.
- *Infrastructure maintenance fund* ($28 million). The Agreement stipulates that the United States make contributions to a fund to be used for maintenance of U.S.-financed major capital improvement projects, including the Compact Road and Airai International Airport.[17] From 2011

through 2024, the U.S. government will contribute $2 million annually, and the Palau government will contribute $600,000 annually to the fund.[18]

- *Fiscal consolidation fund* ($10 million). The Agreement states that the United States shall provide grants of $5 million each in 2011 and 2012, respectively, to help the Palau government reduce its debts. Unless agreed to in writing by the U.S. government, these grants cannot be used to pay any entity owned or controlled by a member of the government or his or her family, or any entity from which a member of the government derives income. U.S. creditors must receive priority, and the government of Palau must report quarterly on the use of the grants until they are expended.

- *Trust fund* ($30.25 million). The Agreement provides for the United States to contribute $30.25 million to the fund from 2013 through 2023. The government of Palau will reduce its previously scheduled withdrawals from the fund by $89 million.[19] From 2024 through 2044, Palau can withdraw up to $15 million annually, as originally scheduled. Moneys from the trust fund account cannot be spent on state block grants, operations of the office of the President of Palau, the Olibiil Era Kelulau (Palau National Congress), or the Palau Judiciary. Palau must use $15 million of the combined total of the trust fund disbursements and direct economic assistance exclusively for education, health, and the administration of justice and public safety.

Annual U.S. assistance to Palau under the Agreement would decline from roughly $28 million in 2011 to $2 million in 2024. Figure 2 details the timeline and composition of assistance outlined in the Agreement.

Agreement Would Continue Compact Federal Services and Extend Framework for Discretionary Federal Programs

The Agreement would extend the authority for the provision of compact federal services and discretionary programs in Palau.

- *Federal services.* The Agreement would amend the compact's subsidiary agreements regarding federal services. The proposed legislation implementing the Agreement would authorize annual appropriations for weather and aviation services. The proposed legislation would also authorize appropriations of $1.5 million to Interior for 2011 through 2024, to subsidize postal services to Palau, the Republic of the Marshall Islands, and the Federated States of Micronesia.

- *Federal discretionary programs.* The Agreement would extend the framework for U.S. agencies to provide discretionary federal programs to Palau and the implementation of these programs is contingent on annual appropriations to those agencies. The implementing legislation would extend the eligibility of the people, government, and institutions of Palau for certain discretionary programs, including special education and Pell grants.

AGREEMENT PROVISIONS WOULD SIGNIFICANTLY IMPROVE PROSPECTS FOR PALAU TRUST FUND

The addition of $30.25 million in U.S. contributions and the delay of $89 million in Palau withdrawals through 2023, as provided by the Agreement, would improve the fund's prospects for sustaining scheduled payments through 2044. At the end of 2010, the fund had a balance of nearly $160 million. Under the Agreement, the trust fund would need a 4.9 percent annual return to yield the proposed withdrawals from 2011 through 2044. This rate is well below the 8.2 percent return it earned from its inception to December 31, 2010.[20] Figure 3 shows projected trust fund balances in 2011 through 2044 under the Agreement, with varying rates of return.

The additional contributions and reduced withdrawals scheduled in the Agreement would also make the trust fund a more reliable source of revenue under conditions of market volatility. With these changes, the trust fund would have an approximately 90 percent probability of sustaining payments through 2044. In comparison, the fund had a 25 percent probability, at the end of 2010, of sustaining the $15 million annual withdrawals scheduled under the compact through 2044.[21]

Figure 4 compares the trust fund's probability of sustaining the proposed withdrawals under the terms outlined in the Agreement with its probability of sustaining the withdrawals scheduled under the compact.

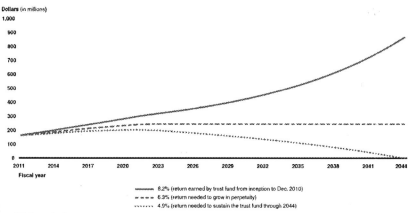

Source: GAO analysis.

Note: The analysis shown is based on the fund's balance as of Dec. 31, 2010, and assumes that the Agreement's provisions related to the trust fund—including additional U.S. contributions and reduced Palau withdrawals through 2023—are approved.

Figure 3. Projected Palau Trust Fund Balance under the Agreement, with Varying Rates of Return, 2011-2044.

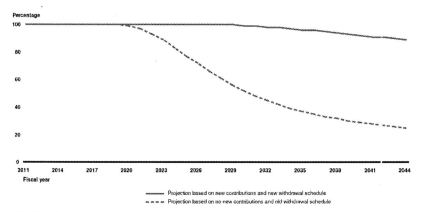

Source: GAO analysis.

Notes: This figure depicts results from 10,000 trial runs. For each run, the returns of each asset class are randomly drawn from a distribution based on the historical returns. The account balances and the withdrawal amount from the trust fund are then calculated based on the returns and the withdrawal schedule. The probability of the trust fund's being able to disburse the scheduled amount is then generated from a distribution of 10,000 disbursements each year.

This figure's upper line shows the probability that the trust fund will sustain scheduled withdrawals under the Agreement's provisions of (1) annual U.S. contributions of $3 million from 2013 through 2022 and $250,000 in 2023 and (2) annual Palau withdrawals of $5 million in 2011, gradually increasing to $13 million in 2023, and $15 million from 2024 through 2044. The figure's lower line shows the probability that the trust fund will sustain scheduled payments under the compact's provision of $15 million annual withdrawals through 2044.

Figure 4. Probability That Palau Trust Fund Will Sustain Scheduled Withdrawals under Two Scenarios.

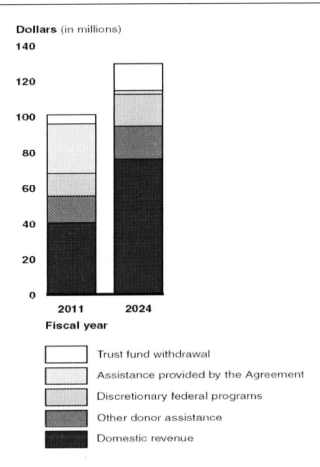

Dollars (in millions)

Trust fund withdrawal

Assistance provided by the Agreement

Discretionary federal programs

Other donor assistance

Domestic revenue

Source: GAO analysis and estimates prepared for the Government of Palau.

Notes:

The years shown were chosen to illustrate the trend in Palau's revenues from 2011, when the terms proposed by the Agreement would begin, through 2024, when assistance provided by the Agreement would expire.

Federal services were not included in the estimates prepared for Palau.

"Trust fund withdrawal" includes the maximum withdrawal for 2011 and 2024 as specified in the Agreement.

"Assistance provided by the Agreement" includes all funding specified in the Agreement.

"Discretionary federal programs" includes estimates prepared for the government of Palau for program funding and grants from U.S. agencies in 2011 and 2024.

"Other donor assistance" includes estimates for assistance from other foreign donors for 2011 and 2024.

"Domestic revenue" includes estimates of taxes and fees to be collected by the Palau government in 2011 and 2024.

Figure 5. Estimated Palau Government Revenues for 2011 and 2024.

ESTIMATES PREPARED FOR PALAU PROJECT DECLINING RELIANCE ON U.S. ASSISTANCE UNDER THE AGREEMENT

Estimates prepared for the government of Palau project that Palau's reliance on U.S. assistance provided under the Agreement will decline, while its reliance on trust fund withdrawals and domestic revenue will increase.[22]

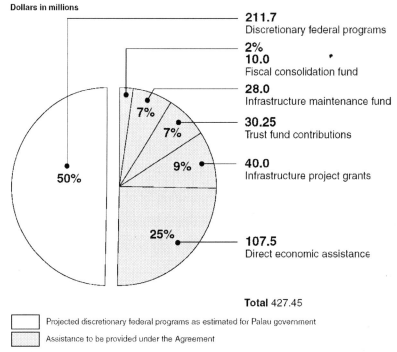

Dollars in millions

211.7
Discretionary federal programs

2%
10.0
Fiscal consolidation fund

28.0
Infrastructure maintenance fund

30.25
Trust fund contributions

40.0
Infrastructure project grants

107.5
Direct economic assistance

7%
7%
9%
50%
25%

Total 427.45

☐ Projected discretionary federal programs as estimated for Palau government

▨ Assistance to be provided under the Agreement

Source: GAO analysis of the Agreement between the Government of the United States of America and the Government of the Republic of Palau Following the Compact of Free Association Section 432 Review, estimates prepared for the Government of Palau.

Notes:

The analysis depicted is based on the estimates prepared for the government of Palau and on the Agreement's provisions. This analysis does not include federal services, which are not addressed in the estimate prepared for Palau and generally are not specified in the Agreement.

"Discretionary federal programs" includes all funds appropriated to federal agencies for assistance to Palau. The discretionary federal program estimates prepared for the government of Palau include annual adjustments for inflation, but not for population growth, from 2009 through 2024. Although the Agreement does not fund discretionary federal programs, it extends authority for U.S. agencies to provide them in Palau subject to annual appropriations.

Figure 6. U.S. Assistance to Palau in 2011-2024 as Estimated for Palau and as Provided under the Agreement.

These estimates show U.S. assistance, as provided under the Agreement, declining from 28 percent of government revenue in 2011 to under 2 percent of government revenue in 2024. The estimates also show Palau's trust fund withdrawals growing from 5 percent of government revenue in 2011 to 12 percent in 2024. In addition, the estimates indicate that Palau's domestic revenue will rise from 40 percent of all government revenues in 2011 to 59 percent in 2024.[23] Finally, the estimates prepared for Palau project a relatively steady reliance on U.S. discretionary federal programs, ranging from 12 percent of all government revenues in 2011 to 14 percent in 2024. The estimates assume that discretionary federal programs will grow at the rate of inflation; however, discretionary programs are subject to annual appropriations and may not increase over time.

Figure 5 shows the types and amounts of Palau's estimated revenues for 2011 and 2024.

Estimates Prepared for Palau Project Discretionary Program Funding as Half of U.S. Assistance

The estimates prepared for the government of Palau project that U.S. assistance to Palau from 2011 through 2024, including discretionary federal programs, will total approximately $427 million. The estimates further project that discretionary programs will account for nearly half of U.S. assistance through 2024, with assistance amounts specified in the Agreement accounting for the other half. (See figure 6.) In contrast, in 2008, we estimated discretionary program funding accounted for less than one-third of total U.S. assistance to Palau in 1995 through 2009.

Chairman Bingaman, Ranking Member Murkowski, and Members of the Committee, this completes my prepared statement. I would be happy to respond to any questions you may have at this time.

STAFF ACKNOWLEDGMENTS

Staff making key contributions to this statement were Emil Friberg, Assistant Director; Ming Chen; Brian Hackney; Reid Lowe; and Grace Lui. Benjamin Bolitzer; Joyce Evans; Mattias Fenton; Farahnaaz Khakoo; Jeremy Sebest; Cynthia Taylor; and Anu Mittal provided technical assistance.

APPENDIX I. U.S. ASSISTANCE TO PALAU PROVIDED UNDER THE COMPACT AND OUTLINED IN THE AGREEMENT

Table 2 illustrates the assistance provided to Palau under the compact from 1995 through 2009. Table 3 illustrates the assistance proposed in the Agreement from 2011 through 2024.

Table 2. Past Compact Assistance Provided to Palau

Dollars in millions																
Types of assistance	1995	1996	1997	1998	1999	2000	2001	2002	2003	2004	2005	2006	2007	2008	2009	Total
Direct assistance	$126.5	$23.5	$22.4	$21.2	$13.6	$13.6	$13.8	$13.9	$14.1	$14.1	$12.7	$12.8	$12.9	$13.0	$13.1	$341.1
Infrastructure	53.0	0	96.0	0	0	0	0	0	0	0	0	0	0	0	0	149.0
Trust fund contributions	66.0	0	4.0	0	0	0	0	0	0	0	0	0	0	0	0	70.0
Total	$245.5	$23.5	$122.4	$21.2	$13.6	$13.6	$13.8	$13.9	$14.1	$14.1	$12.7	$12.8	$12.9	$13.0	$13.1	$560.1

Source: GAO analysis of the Agreement between the U.S. government and the government of the Republic of Palau following the Compact of Free Association Section 432 review.

Table 3. Proposed Assistance in the Agreement

Dollars in millions														
Types of assistance	2011	2012	2013	2014	2015	2016	2017	2018	2019	2020	2021	2022	2023	2024	Total
Trust fund contributions	$0	$0	$3.00	$3.00	$3.00	$3.00	$3.00	$3.00	$3.00	$3.00	$3.00	$3.00	$0.25	$0	$30.25
Infrastructure maintenance fund	2.00	2.00	2.00	2.00	2.00	2.00	2.00	2.00	2.00	2.00	2.00	2.00	2.00	2.00	28.00

Dollars in millions															
Types of assistance	2011	2012	2013	2014	2015	2016	2017	2018	2019	2020	2021	2022	2023	2024	Total
Infrastructure project grants	8.00	8.00	8.00	6.00	5.00	5.00	0	0	0	0	0	0	0	0	40.00
Fiscal consolidation fund	5.00	5.00	0	0	0	0	0	0	0	0	0	0	0	0	10.00
Direct economic assistance	13.00	12.75	12.50	12.00	11.50	10.00	8.50	7.25	6.00	5.00	4.00	3.00	2.00	0	107.50
Total	$28.00	$27.75	$25.50	$23.00	$21.50 S	$20.00	$13.50	$12.25	$11.00	$10.00	$9.00	$8.00	$4.25	$2.00	$215.75

Source: GAO analysis of the Agreement between the U.S. government and the government of the Republic of Palau following the Compact of Free Association Section 432 review.

APPENDIX II. U.S. DISCRETIONARY PROGRAM FUNDS EXPENDED IN 2009

Table 4 lists discretionary U.S. federal program funds expended by the Palau national government, the Palau Community College, and the Palau Community Action Agency, as reported in the organizations' single audit reports for 2009.

Table 4. U.S. Federal Program Expenditure in Palau as Reported in the 2009 Single Audit Reports

U.S. agency	Federal program	2009 expenditure
Agriculture	Cooperative Forestry Assistance	$155,422
Agriculture	Community Facilities Loans and Grants	124,745
Agriculture	Unknown	1,604
Commerce	Special Oceanic and Atmospheric Projects	306,485
Commerce	Unallied Management Projects	1
Education	Pell Grant	2 250,348
Education	Freely Associated States-Education Grant Program	1.309,324
Education	Special Education-Grants to States	859,119
Education	Upward Bound Program	315,164
Education	Talent Search	204,406
Education	Upward Bound Math and Science	198,998
Education	Gaining Early Awareness and Readiness for Undergraduate Programs	198,205
Education	Student Support Services Program	189,771
Education	Special Education-Grants to States	122,755
Education	Federal Work-Study	109,923
Education	Academic Competitiveness Grant	78,346
Education	Supplemental Educational Opportunity Grant	52,600
Education	Byrd Honors Scholarships	46,500
Education	Adult Education-State Grant Program	29,038
HHS	Head Start	1,670,508
HHS	CDC and Prevention-Investigations & Technical Assistance	976,068
HHS	Consolidated Health Centers	564,525
HHS	Substance Abuse and Mental Health Services-Projects of Regional and National Significance	431,171
HHS	National Bioterrorism Hospital Preparedness Program	387,003
HHS	Public Health Emergency Preparedness	343,717
HHS	Epidemiologic Research Studies of AIDS and HIV Infection in Selected Population Groups	260,367
HHS	Material and Child Health Federal Consolidated Programs	201,257
HHS	Family Planning-Services	171,235

U.S. agency	Federal program	2009 expenditure
HHS	Maternal and Child Health Services Block Grant to the States	149,718
HHS	Project Grants and Cooperative Agreements for Tuberculosis Control Programs	116,313
HHS	Immunization Grants	113,372
HHS	Block Grants for Prevention and Treatment of Substance Abuse	111,340
HHS	Universal Newborn Hearing Screening	95,591
HHS	DEH-PHCI	72,266
HHS	Cooperative Agreements to Support Comprehensive School Health Programs to Prevent the Spread of HIV and Other Important Health Problems	67,785
HHS	Basic/Core Area Health and Education Center	62,506
HHS	Block Grants for Community Mental Health Services	58,245
HHS	Consolidated Knowledge Development and Application (KD&A) Program	55,430
HHS	Preventive Health Services - STD Control Grants	48,079
HHS	Cooperative Agreements for State-Based Diabetes Control Programs and Evaluation and Surveillance Systems	44,845
HHS	HIV Care Grants	38,249
HHS	ARRA-Grants to Health Center Programs	20,990
HHS	HIV/Aids Surveillance	19,372
HHS	Preventive Health and Health Services Block Grant	17,375
HHS	Drug Free Communities Support Program Grants	12,759
HHS	Civil Rights and Privacy Rule Compliance Activities	12,620
Interior	Social, Economic and Political Development of the Territories	628,346
Interior	Historical Preservation-Grants in Aid	254,436
Justice	Juvenile Justice and Delinquency Prevention-Allocation to States	1
Labor	ARRA WIA Dislocated Workers Program	128,027
Labor	WIA Dislocated Workers Program	118,574
Labor	ARRA WIA Youth Activities	81,112
Labor	WIA Adult Program	63,241
Labor	WIA Youth Activities	62,637
Labor	ARRA WIA Adult Program	49,162
Transportation	Airport Improvement Program	$4,309,960
Total		**$18,370,956**

Source: GAO analysis of Republic of Palau National Government Independent Auditor's Reports on Internal Control and on Compliance Year Ended September 30, 2009; Palau Community College Comprehensive Annual Financial Report Fiscal Year Ended September 30, 2009; and Palau Community Action Agency Report on the Audit of Financial Statements in Accordance with OMB Circular A-133 Year Ended September 30, 2009.

Note: HHS is the Department of Health and Human Services.

End Notes

[1] *The Agreement between the Government of the United States of America and the Government of the Republic of Palau Following the Compact of Free Association Section 432 Review*, Sept. 3, 2010.

[2] *See* Proclamation 6726, Placing into Full Force and Effect the Compact of Free Association with the Republic of Palau, 59 Fed. Reg. 49777 (Sept. 27, 1994). Congress approved the Compact of Free Association in Public Law 99-658 of Nov. 14, 1986, and Public Law 101-219 of Dec. 12, 1989. The grant funds specified by the compact are backed by the full faith and credit of the U.S. government.

[3] Unless otherwise noted, all years cited are fiscal years (Oct. 1–Sept. 30). In addition, all dollar amounts in this report are in current (i.e., nominal) dollars.

[4] GAO, *Compact of Free Association: Palau's Use of and Accountability for U.S. Assistance and Prospects for Economic Self Sufficiency*, GAO-08-732 (Washington, D.C.: June 10, 2008).

[5] Section 432 of the compact provides for the U.S. and Palau governments to formally review the terms of the compact and its related agreements and to consider the overall nature and development of their relationship, on the 15th, 30th, and 40th anniversaries of the compact's effective date. The governments are to consider the operating requirements of the government of Palau and its progress in meeting the development objectives set forth in section 231(a) of the compact. The terms of the compact shall remain in force until otherwise amended or terminated pursuant to title four of the compact.

[6] The pending bill, Senate Bill 343, amends Title I of Public Law 99-658; approves the results of the 15-year review of the compact, including the Agreement; and appropriates funds for the purposes of the amended Public Law 99-658 for fiscal years ending on or before Sept. 30, 2024, to carry out the agreements resulting from the review.

[7] Palau's private sector relies heavily on foreign workers, mostly from the Philippines. We reported in 2008 that, since 1994, foreign workers, as registered with Palau's Social Security Office, have grown to account for half of Palau's total labor force. Because many of these foreign workers send wage income back to their home nations, in 2005 the annual net outflow of remittances from Palau equaled an estimated 5.5 percent of its GDP.

[8] The International Monetary Fund (IMF) projected that in 2010, Palau's GDP was an estimated $218 million and reported that Palau's GDP per capita was about $10,500. Business and tourist arrivals were projected to be 78,000 in 2010. See IMF, *Republic of Palau Staff Report for the Article IV Consultation* (Apr. 12, 2010).

[9] According to the IMF, in 2010, Palau's public sector spending was projected at approximately 42 percent of its GDP.

[10] The compact's federal programs and services agreement, establishing the legislative framework for the provision of discretionary federal programs in Palau, was in force until Oct. 1, 2009. These services continued under program authority in 2010 and 2011.

[11] GAO-08-732.

[12] Other provisions in the Agreement would define reporting and auditing requirements and passport requirements. The Agreement would require that, by 2018, Palau resolve all deficiencies identified in annual single audit reports, which are required by the Compact's fiscal procedures agreement, such that no single audit report recommendations or deficiencies dating from before 2016 remain. In addition, the Agreement alters the entry procedures for citizens of Palau visiting the United States, requiring them to present a valid machine-readable passport to travel to the United States.

[13] The compact provided for direct assistance to Palau only through 2009. Since then, Interior's 2010 annual budget provided $13.25 million for direct assistance to Palau and other agencies provided additional funds. For 2011, Interior provides $13 million in direct assistance. For 2012, Interior's Budget Justification proposes $29.25 million in direct assistance, while the Agreement provides for $27.75 million.

[14] The pending implementing legislation would also extend the authority, and authorize appropriations, for the provision of compact federal services in Palau. However, the proposed legislation does not appropriate funds for compact federal services.

[15] The Agreement requires that Palau undertake economic, legislative, financial, and management reforms giving due consideration to those identified by the IMF; the Asian Development Bank; and other creditable institutions, organizations, or professional firms.

[16] The compact requires that the United States and Palau consult annually regarding Palau's economic activities and progress in the previous year, as described in a report that Palau must submit each year. Our 2008 report noted that Palau had met reporting conditions associated with direct assistance but that, contrary to compact requirements, the bilateral economic consultations had not occurred on an annual basis; and had been informal and resulted in no written records. See GAO-08-732.

[17] In 2008, we reported that Palau and U.S. officials had expressed concerns about Palau's ability to maintain the Compact Road in a condition that would allow for the desired economic development. We also reported that Palau made initial efforts to maintain the road, but at levels that would cause the road to deteriorate over time and would not provide the economic development benefits envisioned for the people of Palau. See GAO-08-732.

[18] Under the compact, Palau owes the United States a total of $3 million. Under the Agreement, Palau would deposit $3 million in the infrastructure maintenance fund but not expend it. Any future income derived from the $3 million must be used exclusively for the maintenance of the Compact Road.

[19] Under the Agreement, Palau would withdraw $5 million annually through 2013 and gradually increase its maximum withdrawal from $5.25 million in 2014 to $13 million in 2023.

[20] All rates of return on the trust fund are net of fees and commissions unless otherwise noted.

[21] The probability of the fund's sustaining $15 million annual payments through 2044 under the original compact terms has diminished since 2008, when we determined that the probability was 46 percent. See GAO-08-732.

[22] The government of Palau provided fiscal projections through 2024 to the Senate Committee on Energy and Natural Resources in January 2011. The estimates were prepared by an independent economist retained by the government of Palau.

[23] In March 2011, the IMF reported that Palau government revenues as a percentage of GDP are below average for island nations in the Pacific. The report cited opportunities for increased tax revenues by eliminating the gross revenue tax, replacing it with a corporate income tax, introducing a Value Added Tax, and increasing the level of taxation on high earners. The IMF also noted that Palau could reform its civil service to decrease wage expenditures. See IMF, Staff Visit to Republic of Palau–Concluding Statement of the IMF Mission (Mar. 8, 2011)

In: Palau and the Compact of Free Association … ISBN: 978-1-62100-064-8
Editors: J. Berkin and P. D. O'Shaunessy © 2012 Nova Science Publishers, Inc.

Chapter 2

STATEMENT OF H. E. JOHNSON TORIBIONG, PRESIDENT OF THE FREELY ASSOCIATED STATE OF PALAU

H. E. Johnson Toribiong

Chairman Bingaman, Ranking Minority Member Murkowski, and Distinguished Members: Thank you for this opportunity to testify on S. 343, the bill introduced by Senators Bingaman and Murkowski to approve the Agreement Between the United States and Palau reached in the 15th Anniversary Review of the relationship between the United States and Palau and Palau's assistance needs required by Section 432 of the Compact of Free Association between our states. I am here to urge its expeditious approval.

Mr. Chairman, I wrote you in February expressing my deep appreciation for your attention to Palau over the years, your sponsorship of this bill, and your leadership in continuing assistance to our islands while the Congress considers the Agreement. I reiterate this appreciation today.

Senator Murkowski, you are also owed Palau's profound gratitude for your leadership regarding the Agreement.

Committee staff members Allen Stayman and Isaac Edwards are as well.

Palau's thanks apply for the letters that the Committee's bipartisan leadership sent United States executive branch officials asking about the importance of the Compact and the Agreement to United States security interests and requesting a proposed amendment to the legislation to provide the budgetary offset that is needed under United States law and congressional rules to enable the legislation to be considered.

In response, the Departments of Defense and State wrote that the legislation is "vital" to United States security, also using words such as "critical," "increasingly important," and "invaluable." In the words of the Defense Department, a failure to pass it would "jeopardize" United States defense—which understands the situation in Palau. The State Department also wrote that the Department of the Interior has assured that congressional budget requirements would be met.

I hope that the Interior Department makes a proposal for this purpose soon.

To help explain why and why this legislation is needed, I will outline the background of the relationship between the United States and Palau and the Agreement that the bill would approve.

It began with the Battle of the island of Peleliu in 1944 when the United States liberated Palau from Japan in one of the bloodiest battles of World War II. Originally expected to be over in four days, it lasted for more than two months, also resulting in casualties on Angaur and Ngesebus, two other islands of Palau. All told, the United States Armed Forces, consisting of 1st Marine Division, later relieved by the Army's 81st Infantry Division, suffered a total of approximately 9,500 casualties in Palau, including almost 2,000 killed in action.

Through this, valiant Americans liberated Palau from the yoke of colonialism that had weighed heavily on my people for almost 100 years, from the time that the Spanish wrenched freedom from our ancestors, through the era of German rule, and lastly, under the Empire of Japan. Liberation also set in motion events that 50 years later would lead to Palau regaining its sovereignty.

Nevertheless, the gargantuan battle devastated our islands and left our people destitute. Many Palauans were killed. At the end of World War II, fewer than 5,000 Palauans remained alive.

Having taken Palau, the United States governed it; first, under Naval Administration and then as a part of the United Nations Trust Territory of the Pacific Islands. The territory was the U.N. 's only strategic trusteeship at the request of the United States. This made it the only trusteeship subject to U.N. Security Council as well as Trusteeship Council jurisdiction. A Trusteeship Agreement committed the United States to develop Palau socially, economically, and into a self- governing status—but also gave the United States complete control over the islands for which so many Americans had lost their lives and which had tremendous continuing strategic importance to the United States and international peace.

At first, the territory was governed under a policy that closed the islands off from the world, invested little, and only permitted a subsistence economy. As the years went on, however, the United States began to be pressured by the inherent conflict between its obligation to develop Palau into self-government and its desire to maintain military control over a vast, strategic expanse of the Pacific.

The Kennedy Administration's two-pronged solution—continued by succeeding administrations—was, one, to extend substantial assistance, particularly several domestic United States programs, to bind the islands to the United States, and, two, to encourage the idea of free association instead of independence. This status would enable the territory to become self- governing, but retain for the United States full military authority almost as if the islands were United States territory. Compacts of Free Association were negotiated with Palau and two other groups of islands of the Trust Territory.

The Compact with Palau, which was signed in 1985, ultimately made Palau a nation, but gave the United States the desired control over a strategic expanse of the western Pacific the size of Texas between the Philippines, Guam, and Indonesia, as well as military basing rights for 50 years. In consideration, it also committed to give Palau budgetary, developmental, and program assistance, and permits Palauans to enter and work in the United States, as well as to join the United States Armed Forces as—many do.

The Compact as negotiated was not universally embraced in Palau. It took two United States laws, the second enacted in 1989 addressing concerns of many of our people, and seven referenda in Palau before it was finally approved in our islands.

And then it took years to obtain United Nations Security Council approval because of questions as to whether the Compact's United States military rights were more extensive than can exist in another sovereign nation and inconsistent with the fundamental principle of free association.

Palau finally became a state in free association with the United States on October 1st, 1994.

The Compact specified assistance for 15 years and provides, in Section 432, that subsequent assistance for at least the duration of the 50 years of base rights would be determined in periodic joint reviews of Palau's needs. Some of Palau's needs during Years 15 through 50 of free association were to be met through a trust fund. But the framers of the Compact wisely recognized that more would be needed and Palau's needs could not be projected so far into the future. The reviews were also mandated so that both of our freely associated states could re-evaluate the relationship as a whole on a periodic basis. So, the Compact provides for assessments of our association and of the assistance that Palau needs at the 15, 30, and 40-year marks. It also commits the United States to act on the needs of Palau identified in the reviews.

The 15th anniversary of the Compact occurred on October 1, 2009. Because the assistance specified in the Compact was to expire September 30, 2009, Palau sought to begin the 15th Anniversary Review in 2008. However, although some United States officials agreed to take steps in this regard, the effort failed.

The process did not get seriously started until early 2009 when I visited new Secretaries Clinton and Salazar. Then, beginning in May 2009, my Compact Review Advisory Group began to meet with a team of United States representatives led by the Department of State.

The Review was protracted due to delays on the United States side. This necessitated a continuation of assistance to Palau for essential government services in Fiscal Year 2010 based on Fiscal Year 2009 funding which you, Mr. Chairman, others, and, then, the United States Administration requested.

Agreement was finally reached last September 3rd after the personal involvement of Secretary Clinton, Assistant Secretary of the Interior Babauta, Deputy Secretary of the Interior Hayes, then Deputy Secretary of State Lew, Deputy Assistant Secretary of State Reed, and others, and constructive work done by all involved with the United States team.

Senior United States officials encouraged me to sign the Agreement last summer so that it could be approved by the United States Congress in time for Fiscal Year 2011 appropriations. Ultimately, however, it was not submitted to you for approval until this past January. This necessitated another continuation of assistance to Palau for essential services based on Fiscal Year 2009 funding, which I appreciate you, Mr. Chairman, urging and Chairman Inouye of the Appropriations Committee insisting upon.

It also resulted in new requirements regarding the Agreement's approval in the United States Congress. The assistance that the Agreement would provide would be considered mandatory appropriations. Last year's PAYGO Act created a requirement that the cost be offset. New House rules require that the offset be in the form of a reduction in other mandatory spending to make the legislation even eligible for consideration—and leaders of the new House majority have made clear that this is important politically as well.

Under the Agreement, Palau would be provided assistance totaling $215.75 million from Fiscal Years 2011 through 2024—although more than $13 million of this was already appropriated in the continuing appropriations for Fiscal Year 2011.

The total amount is critical for Palau but it is much less than what was provided during the first 15 years of the Compact. In addition, the Agreement would, in response to demands of the United States negotiators, phase out assistance for essential government services and infrastructure by Fiscal Year

2024, with assistance for government services totally ending in Fiscal Year 2023, a year before the next review.

There are other issues: There is no provision to adjust amounts for inflation as in the Compact and the revised compacts with the other freely associated states; the subsidy for the United States Postal Service would continue even if institutes international rates for Palau delivery; and Palau would have to begin paying for audits the United States wants.

The Agreement would also require mutually and expertly determined substantial Palauan spending and revenue reforms. These reforms will require tough measures but are intended— and needed—to strengthen Palau's budgetary practices and its economy. The reforms would ultimately lessen our islands' absolute need for United States assistance. This will create a stronger, more self-reliant Palau, which is what our islands should be and which would be a better partner for the United States.

Finally, the Agreement would also make changes in United States programs and services in response to requests of various United States agencies in areas including civil aviation, postal service, telecommunications, and weather reporting, amending seven of the Compact's subsidiary agreements. The Agreement would, additionally, amend the Compact to reflect Palau's current practice of issuing machine-readable passports, which enhance United States border security.

Strategic control of Palau and its extensive waters and base rights are not all that are at stake for the United States. Our relationship is based upon our common interests and ideals. For example, year in and year out, Palau votes with the United States in the United Nations more than any other member state. It has stood alone with the United States on key votes, including those concerning Israel and Cuba, despite pressure and entreaties from other nations that have offered friendship.

The Government of Palau's agreement to the request of the United States that we provide a home for Chinese Muslims that the Bush Administration determined it had erroneously detained at Guantanamo is another example of the unmatched alliance between Palau and the United States. We agreed to provide this sanctuary when no other nation would. Many Palauans had strong reservations, however, and we also did so over the strong objections of the Government of China, which had made economic overtures to our islands. In fact, Palau has provided third-country refuge to more former Guantanamo detainees than any nation other than predominantly Muslim Albania to assist the United States.

And there is no more telling demonstration of the closeness Palau feels to the United States than the record of Palauans serving in the Armed Forces of the

United States, which I have been told is at a higher rate than any other state of or associated with the United States. Palauans have fought alongside their American comrades-in-arms in Lebanon, Vietnam, Iraq, Afghanistan, and in other theaters of war, and have given their lives and limbs in this service. Just last month, I attended the funeral of another young Palauan who was killed in the Afghanistan. Three of his siblings continue to serve in the United States Army.

Palau is the United States' closest and most loyal ally. The vast majority of Palauans are happy and proud to be able to help the United States and give back to a nation that has done so much for them.

But there are elements that who would use any failure of the United States to live up to its commitments under the Compact to try to diminish the confidence of Palauans and others in the strong relationship between our freely associated states and to encourage Palau in a different direction.

A failure of the United States Congress to approve this Agreement or an undue delay in assistance which now constitutes 24% of Palau's budget would encourage some—including some in Palau who questioned the Compact even when it was approved—to argue that Palau should move away from the United States and look elsewhere.

And if there is no agreement or an end to essential assistance, many Palauans would insist on an end to the United States military rights under the Compact that the Department of Defense has advised are essential to United States security and for maintaining regional peace.

Already some Palauans are enticed by the new economic power of China, which clearly wants more influence in Palau. We all want greater economic interaction with China, but it should be without compromising the close alliance between Palau and the United States

I, personally, have a fundamental and enduring commitment to strengthen the relationship between Palau and the United States. This reflects the real desires of the majority of my people. But we will all face a very serious challenge if this Agreement is not approved, and it is simple logic that United States military rights under the Compact and other Palauan support for the United States under the current association could not be expected to continue if the United States does not continue to meet the promise of the Compact.

The relationship will also be significantly—and very unadvisedly— undermined if assistance that the Government of Palau absolutely needs to continue critical services to its people is allowed to lapse even if the Agreement is subsequently approved by the United States Congress. In this regard, United States officials should plan to continue assistance on at least the current basis if they do not act to enable the Agreement to be approved by United States law soon.

The delay in United States action on the Agreement has already led to substantial questions about it being raised by influential leaders of our island. The danger of the growing doubts should be recognized by United States officials. The history of the Compact in Palau should not be forgotten.

I am, however, hopeful that this hearing will be at a catalyst for the United States executive branch and congressional action needed to approve the Agreement, and am confident that Palau will reflect its appreciation for the United States by approving the Agreement.

I respectfully request the Committee to favorably report the bill and lead the Congress in its enactment.

Thank you for your attention and consideration.

In: Palau and the Compact of Free Association ...   ISBN: 978-1-62100-064-8
Editors: J. Berkin and P. D. O'Shaunessy   © 2012 Nova Science Publishers, Inc.

Chapter 3

TESTIMONY OF FRANKIE REED, DEPUTY ASSISTANT SECRETARY OF STATE, BUREAU OF EAST ASIAN AND PACIFIC AFFAIRS, "COMPACT OF FREE ASSOCIATION WITH THE REPUBLIC OF PALAU: ASSESSING THE 15-YEAR REVIEW"

Frankie Reed

Chairman Bingaman, Senator Murkowski, and Members of the Committee, I am here today to testify on the importance of our bilateral relationship with Palau as well as to discuss the Compact with Palau and proposed legislation approving the results of the mandated 15-year Compact Review. History has proven that this small Pacific island nation remains indispensable to our national security and other core interests in the Pacific. Current and future challenges convince us we must remain steadfast and true to a thriving relationship that delivers much more than it costs in dollars and cents.

Our Compact with Palau was concluded in 1994. It does not have a termination date and requires a review on the 15-year, 30-year, and 40-year anniversaries. Our two governments worked closely over 20 months of negotiations to conclude the 15-year review last September, which resulted in an agreement I signed with President Toribiong. The legislation now proposed to implement the agreement is the outcome of that review and is the manifestation of the shared commitments between our two governments.

The Palau Compact Review legislation amends Title I of Public Law 99-658 regarding the Compact of Free Association between the Government of the United States of America and the Government of Palau. In formal language, this bill approves the results of the 15-year review of the Compact, including the Agreement between our two governments following the Compact of Free Association Section 432 Review. It appropriates funds for the purposes of the amended PL 99-658 for fiscal years ending on or before September 30, 2024, to carry out the agreements resulting from the review.   .

Palau has been and continues to be a strong partner with the United States. Its location on the westernmost point of an arc from California to the Philippines creates a security zone that safeguards U.S. interests in the Pacific. That relationship was born in World War II and has been built over the decades since 1945.

TRANSITION TO INDEPENDENCE

Allow me to look back to the end of World War II. In 1947, the United Nations assigned the United States administering authority over the Trust Territory of the Pacific Islands, which included Palau and island districts of Micronesia that we had liberated from Japanese occupation. During that period, the United States built roads, hospitals and schools and extended eligibility for U.S. federal programs in the Trust Territory. In the following years, the trustee islands sought changes in their political status. Palau adopted its own constitution in 1981, and the governments of the United States and Palau concluded a Compact of Free Association that entered into force on October 1, 1994. The Compact fulfills our solemn commitment to Palau's self-governance in accordance with the freely expressed wishes of the Palauan people. The Compact also provides for an important element of our Pacific strategy for defense of the U.S. homeland and allows us to carry out important foreign policy objectives.

PALAU'S SUPPORT OF THE UNITED STATES

Mr. Chairman, the United States paid dearly in blood in WWII to free Palau. It is a story that every American should understand and that generations before us have seen as creating a sacred trust to remember and honor.

Rising from those ashes, with the strong and steady support of the American people, Palau rebuilt its infrastructure and modeled its government upon the principles of democracy, human rights, and fundamental freedoms. President Toribiong recently signed an Executive Order designating the last Monday of May Memorial Day in Palau, an official holiday. On this day, the people of Palau honor those who paid the ultimate sacrifice to defend the freedom and democratic principles we all enjoy today. On May 30, President Toribiong and our U.S. Ambassador to Palau laid wreaths on the grounds of the WW II monument in Peleliu State. More than 2,000 American soldiers lost their lives and more than 10,000 were wounded in the Battle of Peleliu, one of the bloodiest battles of WW II. Palau remains a strong reliable partner and continues to share our values through these historic ties.

The United States can count on Palau to vote with us on controversial issues in multilateral fora. On a number of important resolutions in the General Assembly over the past year, Palau stood by us and provided critical votes. For example, Palau has voted with the United States on controversial resolutions related to Israel 100 percent of the time and on human rights issues, 93 percent of the time. Palau's overall voting coincidence with us is at 87 percent.

Although Palau is a steadfast and committed friend of the United States, China, the Arab states, Cuba and others are actively courting Palau, and the other Pacific island nations, as they seek to build influence in the region. The United States must maintain and strengthen its relationship with Palau by maintaining our strong friendship and upholding our commitments as set forth in the Compact.

The results of the 15-year Compact Review as reflected in the subsequent legislation nurture our unique relationship. By supporting the Compact Trust Fund, the United States contributes to Palau's development and secures our security interests. Our contribution represents a vital link between our two countries. Implementation of the results of the Compact review sends a reassuring signal to Palau and others in the Pacific region and beyond that the United States follows through on its commitments, in good times and in difficult times. These are indeed difficult times for us. However, it is essential to our long-term national interests to make sure that the United States remains true to its identity as a Pacific power. Meeting vital interests more than six decades ago, the United States invested blood and treasure. Today, it remains in our strategic, political and economic interests to nurture Palau's young democracy, support its development, and increase its self-sufficiency.

U.S. Defense Interests in Palau

Mr. Chairman, the United States and the people of the Pacific have fought side-byside. Our identity as a "Pacific power" was, in many ways, forged on the beaches of the Pacific during World War II.

The importance of our special relationship with Palau is most clearly manifested in the U.S. defense posture in the Asia–Pacific region, which forms a north-south arc from Japan and South Korea to Australia. Maintaining U.S. primacy in the Pacific depends on our strong relationship with the Freely Associated States of Palau, the Marshall Islands and the Federated States of Micronesia, which along with Hawaii, Guam, the Commonwealth of the Northern Mariana Islands, American Samoa and the smaller U.S. territories comprise an invaluable east-west strategic security zone that spans almost the entire width of the Pacific Ocean.

Additionally, critical security developments in the region require the United States' sustained presence and engagement, particularly given the range of U.S. strategic interests and equities in the Western Pacific. Essential elements of our presence include the Reagan Ballistic Missile Defense Test Site on U.S. Army Kwajalein Atoll and disaster relief operations throughout the region. This posture will become increasingly important as regional powers become increasingly active and seek to supplant U.S. military leadership and economic interests in the region. Following through on our commitments to Palau, as reflected in the proposed legislation, buttresses our defense posture in the Western Pacific.

Palau does not maintain its own military forces, but under the terms of our Compacts, their citizens are eligible to serve in the U.S. Armed Forces. And they do. Palauan citizens volunteer in the U.S. military at a rate higher than in any individual U.S. state. Approximately 200 Palauan men and women serve in our military today, out of a population of about 14,000. Palau is indeed a strong partner who punches well above its weight. We are grateful for their sacrifices and dedication to promoting peace and fighting terrorism. Palau has deployed soldiers for U.S. coalition missions and participated in U.S.-led combat operations in the world's most difficult and dangerous places. Since 9/11, at least six Palauans lost their lives in combat.

Just this year, Sgt. Sonny Moses was killed in Afghanistan while serving with his comrades providing computer training to Afghan citizens. Sgt. Moses was the youngest of eight children of Mr. and Mrs. Sudo Moses and when his body came to Palau for burial, three of his siblings came home in U.S. uniform. Of the family of eight, four chose to serve in the United States military. And during the motorcade for his procession to the Capitol the streets of Koror were lined with citizens waving U.S. and Palauan flags. This sad occasion shows just how close the ties between the United States and Palau truly are.

President Toribiong's niece and Minister Jackson Ngiraingas' son both serve in the U.S. Navy. The son of Minoru Ueki, Palau's Ambassador to Japan, serves in our army. Palau Paramount Chief Reklai has a daughter and son in the Army. Palau's Ambassador to the United States Hersey Kyota has two adult children serving in the Armed Forces. He has several nephews serving in the Army and Marine Corps. Similarly, many other Palauan sons and daughters of other government officials and of ordinary Palauan citizens served honorably in U.S. military units over the past decades and most recently in Afghanistan and Iraq.

The Compact and our continued commitment to Palau, as manifested in the proposed legislation, will reinforce an important element of our Pacific strategy for defense of the U.S. homeland. As you will hear from Deputy Assistant Secretary of Defense Robert Scher, the U.S.-Palau Compact includes provisions that close Palau to the military forces of any nation, except the United States. The United States enjoys access to Palauan waters, lands, airspace, and its Exclusive Economic Zones (EEZ), a vital asset for our defense and security needs. Our relationship with Palau allows the United States to guard its long-term defense interests in the region.

Beyond Defense Interests

The importance of our strong relationship with Palau extends beyond defense considerations. Palau works closely with the U.S. to detect and combat international crime and terror. In 2009, Palau resettled six ethnic Uighur detainees from Guantanamo at a time when few other countries were willing to step up. Palau was the first island partner to sign the U.S. Coast Guard ship rider and ship boarding agreements that bolster law enforcement in the vast Pacific region.

Our people-to-people ties continue to grow. Since 1966, more than 4,200 Peace Corps Volunteers taught English, offered life skills education, and supported economic development, education, capacity building, and marine and terrestrial resource conservation in Palau and in the two other Freely Associated States. Today approximately 55 Peace Corps volunteers serve in Micronesia and Palau.

THE ADMINISTRATION'S PACIFIC STRATEGY

Mr. Chairman, the President, Secretary Clinton, and others in this Administration deeply appreciate the historic World War II legacy of the Pacific and the strategic role it plays, particularly in keeping the Pacific Islands allied with the United States. Today, we find ourselves in a tumultuous global political environment that calls for wisdom and long-term strategic vision. An investment in Palau today will help to ensure Palau will continue to stand with us as a staunch, dependable, democracy tomorrow.

Palau is Important, But Why Enact the U.S.-Palau Legislation Now?

Palau's stable government is modeled on our own. Palau shares our vision on important international goals for human rights and democracy. The maturity of the democratic process in as relatively young a state as Palau is a testament to the strong values of the people of the Pacific and reinforces the value of the Compact as a vehicle for their transition to greater self-sufficiency.

Palau was the first insular area, including the U.S. territories, to get a clean audit opinion on the government's financial statements. Public facilities are in good repair, and Palau puts a great deal of care into maintaining a pristine environment, especially by addressing critical areas of energy, water, sewer, and transportation. They understand the importance of continuing efforts to operate within a balanced budget.

We must remain true to our commitment to the people of Palau. The bottom line is that Palau is an irreplaceable and loyal partner, who shares our interests in preserving regional and international security. Failing to affirm the results of the 15-year review of the Compact with Palau is not in our national interest. We appreciate the interest and leadership of this Committee in considering this legislation promptly and hope both the Senate and the House will pass it this session.

Although the Department of the Interior is responsible for implementing and funding the Compact programs, I would like to say a few words about the assistance package resulting from the 15-year review. The direct economic assistance provisions of the Compact expired on September 30, 2009. The outcome of the 15-year review resulted in an assistance agreement that provides $215.75M to Palau over the next 14 years and enables Palau to transition to reliance on a $15 million a year withdrawal from its trust fund; instead of the $13 million in direct assistance and \$5 million from its trust fund that it has come to rely on, The assistance package included in the legislation, which provides approximately \$215 million to Palau divided over the next 14 years, reflects an effort to ease Palau off of U.S. direct economic assistance as it continues to grow and reform its economy. As a result of the Compact review, Palau will have continued eligibility for a wide range of Federal programs and services from agencies such as the U.S. Postal Service, federal weather services, the Federal Aviation Administration, the Department of Agriculture, and Health and Human Services.

If the bilateral agreement between our two countries is not implemented, the trust fund would be unable to provide a steady outlay of \$15 million a year from now until 2044, which was the intended purpose of the Compact negotiators in the 1980s. The Trust Fund suffered considerable shrinkage as a result of the recent global financial crisis. For the smooth continuation of our bilateral relationship, it is crucial that we provide Palau the assistance agreed to in the Compact review.

Mr. Chairman, in closing I would like to emphasize that Palau, a small island country far away in the Pacific, was our protectorate and is now our ally. The people of Palau are woven into the American fabric, serving with distinction and honor in our military and living and working beside us in the United States. Thanks to its geography, Palau is a unique outpost in our security arc in the Pacific. It is a place America liberated with its blood and that now helps us protect the western flank of our homeland. The economic center of gravity continues to shift to the Asia Pacific, and the vital importance of a stable, increasingly prosperous and democratic Palau to U.S. interests in this dynamic region continue to grow.

I hope that my testimony today, coupled with that of my colleagues from the Department of the Interior and the Department of Defense, has given you a more robust and complete picture of the key role played by the Compact in not only cementing our partnership with Palau, but also in serving the interests of the United States.

I look forward to working with you and other Members of Congress to secure and advance U.S. interests in Palau by passing the legislation implementing the results of the Compact review.

Thank you again for giving me the opportunity to testify before you today and to clarify the importance of this legislation. I look forward to answering your questions.

In: Palau and the Compact of Free Association …   ISBN: 978-1-62100-064-8
Editors: J. Berkin and P. D. O'Shaunessy   © 2012 Nova Science Publishers, Inc.

Chapter 4

STATEMENT OF ANTHONY M. BABAUTA, ASSISTANT SECRETARY OF THE INTERIOR-INSULAR AREAS, DEPARTMENT OF THE INTERIOR, "THE AGREEMENT BETWEEN THE GOVERNMENT OF THE UNITED STATES OF AMERICA AND THE GOVERNMENT OF THE REPUBLIC OF PALAU FOLLOWING THE COMPACT OF FREE ASSOCIATION, SECTION 432 REVIEW"

Anthony M. Babauta

Chairman Bingaman and members of the Committee on Energy and Natural Resources, I am pleased to be here today to discuss S. 343, a bill that would amend Public Law 99-658 and approve the results of the review of fifteen-years of the Compact of Free Association between the Government of the United States and the Government of the Republic of Palau (ROP). My colleagues from the Departments of State and Defense will discuss the importance of the United States - Palau relationship as it relates to national security and our policies in the Pacific. My statement today will focus on the financial assistance components of the new agreement with Palau for which the Department of the Interior will be responsible.

THE UNITED STATES – PALAU RELATIONSHIP

The Department of the Interior and the Government of Palau have been partners since 1951, when the Navy transferred to the Department of the Interior the administration of the United Nations Trust Territory of the Pacific Islands. Since the end of World War II, Palau has emerged from its status as a war-ravaged protectorate to become a sovereign nation and member of the world community. Consistent with the provisions of the 1994 Compact of Free Association, Palau has exercised its sovereignty in accordance with the principles of democracy and in a firm alliance with the United States.

The Compact of Free Association has proven to be a very successful framework for United States – Palau relations. The goals of the first fifteen years of the Compact have been met: the trusteeship was terminated; Palau's self-government was restored; a stable democratic state was established; third countries were denied military influence in the region of Palau; and with United States financial assistance, a base for economic growth has been provided.

The original financial terms and conditions of the Compact have been fully implemented by the United States and Palau. The United States, through the Department of the Interior, has provided over $600 million of assistance including $149 million used to construct the 53-mile road system on the island of Babeldoab and $38.7 million for health care and education block grants. Most of the funding, $400 million, was expended on activities defined under Title Two of the Compact, which included general government operations, energy production, communications, capital improvements, health and education programs and establishment of the Compact Trust Fund.

The Compact Trust Fund was an important feature of U.S. assistance. Capitalized with $70 million during the first three years of the agreement in the 1 990s, the objective of the trust fund was to produce an average annual amount of $15 million as revenue for Palau government operations for the thirty-five year period fiscal year 2010 through fiscal year 2044. The fund also generated $5 million in annual operational revenue for Palau since the fourth year of the agreement, totaling $60 million for the years 1998 through 2009.

Palau has made strong economic gains under the Compact of Free Association. Its growth, in real terms, has averaged just over 2 percent per year. Palau's governmental services are meeting the needs of its community. Palau has taken control of its destiny and is moving in the right direction.

COMPACT REVIEW

As both the United States and Palau began the required Compact section 432 review several years ago, each side took pride in the growth evident in Palau. However, the review, which examined the terms of the Compact and its related agreements and the overall nature of the bilateral relationship, also focused attention on several important issues. The United States and Palau agreed that prospects for continued economic growth relied on four key factors: 1) the viability of the Compact trust fund and its ability to return $15 million a year; 2) the implementation of fiscal reforms to close the gap between Palau's revenues and expenditures by shrinking its public sector and raising revenue; 3) the promotion of increased foreign investment and private sector growth, and, 4) the continuation of certain United States assistance, including access to United States Federal domestic programs and services.

From the perspective of the United States, the viability of the Compact Trust Fund was of paramount concern. The economies of Pacific islands are always fragile; their size, distance from markets and relative lack of resources make growth a perennial problem. Although Palau has some relative advantages in contrast to other Pacific island countries, the Compact Trust Fund was established with the intention of providing a relatively secure revenue base for Palau's government through fiscal year 2044. As the 15-year review began, Palau's trust fund, which had earned roughly 9 percent annually since its inception, had suffered significant losses. As GAO reported in 2008, it was uncertain that the trust fund could pay $15 million annually to the Government of Palau through fiscal year 2044.

COMPACT AGREEMENT

The condition of the Compact Trust Fund, the need for fiscal and economic reforms, and the goal of strengthening conditions for private sector growth became the focus of the bilateral review. I believe that the *Agreement Between the Government of the United States of America and the Government of the Republic of Palau Following the Compact of Free Association Section 432 Review* (Agreement) that arose from the 15-year review, and which is embodied in S. 343 will address these concerns, maintain stability, promote economic growth and increase the progress already made under the Compact of Free Association.

The Agreement extends United States assistance, in declining annual amounts, through fiscal year 2024. The total of direct financial assistance to Palau under the Agreement is $229 million, although $13.1 million of that amount has already been appropriated for direct economic assistance by congressional action in fiscal year 2010 and $13 million in fiscal year 2011.

Under the Agreement, in 2011 the United States is to provide Palau $28 million (of which $13 million is the aforementioned direct assistance), and the amount will decline every year thereafter. The declining amount of assistance is intended to provide an incentive for Palau to develop other sources of local revenue and serves notice that the Palauan government has agreed that it will need to make systemic adjustments to its government in order to live within those same resources.

The Agreement contains five categories of financial assistance to Palau.

Direct economic assistance. The Agreement provides for direct assistance for education, health, administration of justice and public safety, in amounts starting at $13 million in 2011, declining to $2 million, the last payment, in 2023. The timing of direct assistance payments is conditioned on Palau's making certain fiscal reform efforts. If the United States government determines that Palau has not made meaningful progress in implementing meaningful reforms, direct assistance payments may be delayed until the United States Government determines that Palau has made sufficient progress on the reforms.

Infrastructure projects. Under the Agreement the United States is to provide grants to Palau for mutually agreed infrastructure projects—$8 million in 2011 through 2013, $6 million in 2014, and $5 million in both 2015 and 2016. The Agreement does not name any projects.

Infrastructure maintenance fund. Under the Agreement, a trust fund will be established to be used for maintenance of capital projects previously financed by the United States, including the existing Compact Road. From 2011 through 2024, the United States government will contribute $2 million annually and the Palau government will contribute $600,000 annually to the fund. This will protect crucial United States investments in Palau that significantly contribute to economic development.

Fiscal consolidation fund. The United States will provide grants of $5 million each in 2011 and 2012 to help the Palau government reduce its debt. United States creditors must receive priority, and the government of Palau must report quarterly on the use of the grants until they are expended. This fund will also simplify needed economic adjustments to Palau's fiscal policies.

Trust fund. The Agreement increases the size of Palau's trust fund directly and indirectly to bolster the likelihood that the trust fund will yield payments of up to $15 million annually through 2044. First, the United States will contribute $3 million annually from 2013 through 2022 and contribute $250,000 in 2023. Second, the government of Palau will delay withdrawals from the fund, drawing $5 million annually through 2013 and gradually increasing its withdrawal ceiling from $5.25 million in 2014 to $13 million in 2023. From 2024 through 2044, Palau is expected to withdraw up to $15 million annually, as originally scheduled. Under the Agreement, withdrawals from the trust fund may only be used for education, health, administration of justice and public safety.

CONTINUING COOPERATION

The United States and Palau will work cooperatively on economic reform. The Agreement requires the two governments to establish an advisory group to recommend economic, financial and management reforms. Palau is committed to adopting and implementing reforms. Palau will be judged on its progress in such reforms as the elimination of operating deficits, reduction in its annual budgets, reducing the number of government employees, implementing meaningful tax reform and reducing subsidies to public utilities.

Palau's progress in implementing reforms will be addressed at annual bilateral economic consultations. If the government of the United States determines that Palau has not made significant progress on reforms, the United States may delay payment of economic assistance under the Agreement.

The Agreement also continues to provide other United States services and grant programs, including the United States Postal Service, the National Weather Service, and the Federal Aviation Administration. The Postal Service moves mail between the United States and Palau, and offers other related services. Palau maintains its own postal service for internal mail delivery. The National Weather Service reimburses Palau for the cost of operating its weather station in Palau, which performs upper air observations twice daily, as requested, for the purpose of Palau's airport operations and the tracking of cyclones that may affect other United States territories, such as Guam. The Federal Aviation Administration provides aviation services to Palau, including en-route air traffic control from the mainland United States, flight inspection of airport navigation aids, and technical assistance and training.

The proposed legislation will also allow the continuance of other Federal program services currently available to Palau under separate authorizing legislation, including programs of the Departments of Education and Health and Human Services. The general authorization for Palau to receive such services was created by the Compact, but individual program eligibility has been created by specific laws that include Palau as an eligible recipient.

The Palau Compact legislative proposal does have PAYGO costs. These costs are included in the President's Budget along with a number of legislative proposals with PAYGO savings. Some proposals that fall under this Committee's jurisdiction include:

- Net Receipt Sharing, which takes into account the costs of managing Federal oil and gas leases before revenues are shared with the States;
- Terminate payments for reclaiming abandoned coal mines to states that are already certified as having cleaned up all of their priority sites; and
- Production incentive fees on non-producing Federal oil and gas leases.

Each example by itself could provide more than enough savings to offset the costs of the Palau Compact. These proposals are also viable; Net Receipt Sharing, for example, has been enacted for four years through annual appropriations language.

The Administration looks forward to continuing our partnership with Palau. The Department of the Interior is proud of the positive advancements our assistance to Palau has provided over the last fifteen years and looks forward to the progress that we anticipate will be made over the next fifteen years.

In: Palau and the Compact of Free Association ...   ISBN: 978-1-62100-064-8
Editors: J. Berkin and P. D. O'Shaunessy   © 2012 Nova Science Publishers, Inc.

Chapter 5

TESTIMONY OF ROBERT SCHER, DEPUTY ASSISTANT SECRETARY OF DEFENSE, SOUTH AND SOUTHEAST ASIA, "DEPARTMENT OF DEFENSE'S SUPPORT OF THE PALAU COMPACT AGREEMENT REVIEW"

Robert Scher

INTRODUCTION

Members of the Committee, thank you for the opportunity to appear before you to discuss the importance of the Palau Compact Agreement. Since its enactment in 1994, the Compact has served as an important foundation for our security strategy in the Asia-Pacific region, providing the United States with critical access, influence, and strategic denial of access to other regional militaries. Our Compact with Palau, coupled with our compacts with the Federated States of Micronesia (FSM) and the Republic of the Marshall Islands (RMI), has enabled DoD to maintain critical access and influence in the Asia-Pacific region. Passage of S. 343, a bill to amend Title I of PL 99-658 regarding the Compact of Free Association between the United States and Palau, is vital to allowing the Department to continue to benefit from the security arrangement afforded by the Compact. Today, I would like to take the opportunity to discuss the importance of Palau and the Compact to preserving U.S. national security interests in the Asia- Pacific region.

PALAU 'S CONTRIBUTIONS TO AMERICAN AND GLOBAL SECURITY

Let me begin by discussing Palau in the context of the regional security environment in the Western Pacific. The Pacific Islands region is sparsely populated, physically isolated, and geographically widespread. However, Palau lies at a pivotal crossroad in the Pacific, an area near critical sea lines of communication and rich fishing grounds. It is also located directly in the so-called "Second Island Chain" from Mainland Asia, close to all of the major East and Southeast Asian powers. With our strategic interests and equities expanding in shifting more toward the Asia-Pacific region, having Palau as a strong partner in the Pacific is increasingly important to maintaining military, as well as political and diplomatic, leadership in this quickly evolving strategic environment.

We must take note of critical security developments in the Pacific that require the Department's sustained presence and engagement. Broadly speaking, countries such as China, Russia, and the Arab states are actively courting Pacific Island States, challenging the security status quo in the region, and increasing their economic, diplomatic, and military engagement with the island States. These critical security developments require sustained U.S. presence and engagement in the region. Our relationship with Palau under the Compact would be reinforced with passage of this legislation and would ensure the United States the extraordinary advantage to deny other militaries access to Palau. For these reasons, it is imperative that the U.S. Government sustain this advantage.

Since the Compact of Free Association between the Government of the United States of America and the Government of Palau went into effect in 1994, the United States has taken full responsibility for the security and defense of Palau. This unique security arrangement has created a steadfast and reliable partner that helps the United States advance its national security goals in the region.

PALAU IN THE REGIONAL SECURITY CONTEXT

I would also like to highlight the extraordinary service of Palauans in the U.S. Armed Forces and contributions to U.S. security. Under the provisions of the Compact, Palauans are able to serve in the U.S. Armed Forces. In fact, Palauans serve in the U.S. Armed Forces in impressive numbers. Sadly, five Palauans have made the ultimate sacrifice, and numerous others wounded, fighting on the battlefield in Afghanistan and Iraq since 9/11. Their sacrifice in the defense of the U.S. homeland and U.S. and Coalition security interests should not go unnoticed. Furthermore, in 2009, Palau stepped up to offer resettlement to six Uighur detainees from Guantanamo Bay at a time when other countries were hesitant to take these individuals.

Most notably, our commitment to the Compact with Palau allows the Department to leverage Palau's strategic geopolitical position to sustain U.S. security interests in the region. The United States exercises full authority over and responsibility for the security and defense of Palau, an arrangement similar to those that we have with the Federated States of Micronesia and the Republic of the Marshall Islands. With this authority and responsibility, the United States is entitled to military access to the lands, water, and airspace of Palau and retains the right to deny such access to the military forces of other nations. Our current security arrangement affords us expansive access, which will be an increasingly important asset in the defense and security interests of the United States in the Asia-Pacific region in coming years. The Department recognizes the strategic value of the Compact, and we hope to continue to utilize it to serve our national security interests.

U.S.-PALAU DEFENSE RELATIONS

We have growing national security interests and equities in the Western Pacific, a region that is traditionally overlooked and undervalued. Together with the two other Compact States, the Federated States of Micronesia and the Republic of the Marshall Islands, Palau forms part of an important security zone under exclusive U.S. control that spans the entire width of the Pacific when we include Hawaii and the U.S. territories, Guam and the Commonwealth of the Northern Mariana Islands. Palau's location makes it an important part of the U.S. strategic presence in the Asia-Pacific. The Palau Compact affords us strategic positioning in a country with a unique geopolitical position in the Asia-Pacific.

The region's lack of political and security infrastructure has given rise to a trend of growing transnational crime, which underscores the importance of continued DoD engagement in the Western Pacific. With this in mind, the Department seeks to develop creative ways to remain strategically engaged in the region. Recognizing that Palau has no military and only limited law enforcement capabilities and resources, the Department's engagement with Palau primarily focuses on helping them develop maritime security and humanitarian assistance capabilities.

First, maritime security has been one of the most fruitful areas of cooperation between our two nations. DoD sends mobile training teams to Palau to help train local security personnel in maritime security-related matters. Palau's EEZ is part of the Pacific's richest fishing grounds and has traditionally faced serious problems with foreign exploitation of the fishery resources. Large numbers far-ranging fishing vessels from other pacific nations threaten encroachment. Japan, China, Taiwan, and the United States participate in a highly competitive multi-million dollar tuna industry. The Department is currently reviewing ways to use existing DoD assets and cooperative mechanisms to enhance maritime domain awareness in the region.

To combat illegal fishing, the U.S. Coast Guard has entered into a shiprider agreement with Palau, which enables Palauan security officials to embark on transiting U.S. Coast Guard vessels to conduct maritime patrol of its enormous, under patrolled Exclusive Economic Zone (EEZ). This kind of shiprider agreement allows the U.S. Coast Guard to play a more active role in developing partner law enforcement capacity of the island States. In addition, we are cooperating with Japan, Australia, Palau, the Marshall Islands, and Micronesia to bring to fruition the Sasakawa Peace Foundation's $10 million initiative to support maritime surveillance in all three Compact States.

Second, the Department's humanitarian programs have been very well-received in island communities. These programs primarily focus on the removal of explosive remnants of war from the World War II era, humanitarian projects, and prisoner of war/missing in action operations. DoD's 12-person Civic Action Team maintains a rotational presence in Palau, conducting small- to medium-scale humanitarian and civic action projects in the health, education, and infrastructure areas. Especially notable are the large-scale, multinational, pre-planned humanitarian missions, the U.S. Air Force's Pacific Angel and U.S. Navy's Pacific Partnership, which include medical and engineering projects in remote regions that are conducted in close coordination with local communities. In the summer of 2010, more than 1,900 Palauans were treated, 14 community service projects were completed, and more than 1,000 man hours spent across the three states of Koror, Peleliu and Angaur when USS BLUE RIDGE (LCC-19) stopped in Palau as part of Pacific Partnership 2010. Also, the longest running humanitarian campaign in the world, Operation Christmas Drop, which provides air-dropped supplies to the people of the remote Micronesian islands each December, celebrated its 58th anniversary in December 2010 and continues annually to assist the remote islands of Palau. These humanitarian missions are evidence that the Department's engagement in Palau extends well beyond traditional security parameters.

CONCLUSION

In conclusion, U.S. power projection in the Asia-Pacific region will continue to be essential to our national security interests. The U.S.-Palau Compact is a strategic asset for U.S. presence in the Western Pacific, an increasingly important region. Loss of the defense rights and exclusive access granted to the United States under the Compact would adversely affect U.S. national security. Our relationship with Palau is unique and reliable. Passage of the proposed legislation approving the results of the 15- year Compact Review would ensure this important security agreement continues and would reassure Palau of our sustained commitment to Palau and its people and of our shared interest in regional and global security. I urge you to support the continued security agreement the United States has developed with Palau over the years and ask for your support of the proposed legislation.

In: Palau and the Compact of Free Association …   ISBN: 978-1-62100-064-8
Editors: J. Berkin and P. D. O'Shaunessy   © 2012 Nova Science Publishers, Inc.

Chapter 6

COMPACT OF FREE ASSOCIATION: PALAU'S USE OF AND ACCOUNTABILITY FOR U.S. ASSISTANCE AND PROSPECTS FOR ECONOMIC SELF-SUFFICIENCY

United States Government Accountability Office

WHY GAO DID THIS STUDY

The Compact of Free Association between the Republic of Palau and the United States entered into force on October 1, 1994, with the U.S. interest of promoting Palau's self-sufficiency and economic advancement. The compact and its related subsidiary agreements provide for a 15-year term of economic assistance. In fiscal year 2009, the two governments must review the terms of the compact and related agreements and agree on any modifications. The Department of the Interior (DOI) has primary responsibility for oversight of Palau's use of compact funds. GAO was requested to report on (1) the provision of compact and other U.S. assistance to Palau in fiscal years 1995-2009; (2) Palau's and U.S. agencies' efforts to provide accountability over Palau's use of federal funds in 1995-2006; and (3) Palau's prospects for achieving economic self-sufficiency. GAO reviewed Palau's compact annual reports, financial statements and internal control reports for fiscal years 1995-2006, as well as other compact-related documentation. GAO interviewed officials from the U.S. and Palau governments and conducted fieldwork in Palau.

WHAT GAO RECOMMENDS

GAO recommends that the Secretary of the Interior direct the Office of Insular Affairs to formally consult with the government of Palau regarding Palau's financial management challenges and assist Palau in building financial management capacity. DOI and Palau agreed with GAO's recommendations.

WHAT GAO FOUND

For fiscal years 1995-2009, U.S. aid to Palau is expected to exceed $852 million. Compact direct assistance will account for 48 percent of U.S. assistance; this assistance provides general budgetary support for Palau's government operations, including initial investment in a trust fund intended to provide annual distributions of $5 million in 1999-2009 and $15 million in 2010-2044. Compact federal services such as postal, aviation, and weather services will account for about 3 percent of assistance, and construction of a road, finished in 2007, will account for 17 percent of assistance. Palau's receipt of federal programs, providing services such as education grants and community health care, will account for approximately 31 percent of assistance.

Single audit reports for fiscal years 1995-2006 show that Palau has made progress in its financial accountability through improvements in the timeliness and reliability of its financial statements. However, the reports show that Palau has persistent internal control weaknesses over financial reporting and over compliance with laws and regulations governing federal grants. According to Palau officials, inadequate capacity in financial accounting resources and expertise limits Palau's ability to address these weaknesses in a timely way. These weaknesses put at risk Palau's ability to sustain its progress in financial accountability and to operate a major federal program according to applicable requirements. Palau met most compact and subsidiary agreement accountability requirements. However, although DOI used single audit reports and Palau's compact annual reports to monitor Palau's use of compact funds, DOI's oversight was lacking in some matters.

Palau's prospects for economic self-sufficiency depend on four key factors:

- **Levels of continued U.S. assistance.** Given the $10 million scheduled increase in Palau's annual trust fund withdrawals in fiscal year 2010, the expiration of $13.3 million in compact direct assistance will likely reduce

Palau's national government revenues by less than 4 percent. However, future levels of discretionary federal programs—estimated at $11.9 million in 2009—could have a more significant fiscal impact. Also, unless compact federal services are extended, Palau will lose services funded by U.S. agencies estimated to cost almost $1.6 million in 2009.

- **Availability and value of trust fund distributions.** Palau's trust fund can distribute $15 million per year for 35 years if it earns a compounded annual return of at least 8.1 percent, a rate lower than the average earned thus far. However, market volatility could lead to the trust fund's depletion after 2016. Moreover, inflation will cause the distributions to lose value over time.

- **Fiscal reform.** To reduce its reliance on trust fund financing, Palau will require fiscal reforms to increase revenues and decrease expenditures.

- **Private sector growth.** Palau will need to improve its business environment by addressing problems with its foreign investment climate; financial system; and land, labor, and commercial policies that currently discourage private sector growth.

ABBREVIATIONS

ADB	Asian Development Bank
CAT	Civic Action Team
DOD	Department of Defense
DOT	Department of Transportation
Education	Department of Education
FAA	Federal Aviation Administration
FAC	Federal Audit Clearinghouse
FASEG	Freely Associated States Education Grant
FSM	Federated States of Micronesia
GDP	gross domestic product
HHS	Department of Health and Human Services
IMF	International Monetary Fund
Interior	Department of the Interior
OIA	Office of Insular Affairs
OIG	Office of the Inspector General
OMB	Office of Management and Budget
PNCC	Palau National Communications Corporation
NWS	National Weather Service

RMI	Republic of the Marshall Islands
SEPPIE	Special Education Program for Pacific Island Entities
State	Department of State
USACE	U.S. Army Corps of Engineers
USDA	Department of Agriculture
USPS	U.S. Postal Service

June 10, 2008   •

The Honorable Jeff Bingaman
Chairman
The Honorable Pete V. Domenici
Ranking Member
Committee on Energy and Natural Resources
United States Senate

The Honorable Donna M. Christensen
Chairwoman
The Honorable Luis G. Fortuño
Ranking Member
Subcommittee on Insular Affairs
Committee on Natural Resources
House of Representatives

The Compact of Free Association between the Republic of Palau and the United States entered into force on October 1, 1994, with the U.S. interest of promoting Palau's self-sufficiency and economic advancement. The compact and its related subsidiary agreements established a 15-year term of economic assistance and specified security and defense relations between Palau and the United States. Since 1995,[1] U.S. aid to Palau has included assistance provided for in the compact—direct assistance from 1995 through 2009, including investment in a trust fund intended to produce an annual distribution of $15 million from 2010 through 2044; federal services; and construction of a major road—as well as discretionary federal programs.[2] The compact's fiscal procedures subsidiary agreement[3] requires an annual audit of Palau's use of compact funds. The agreement also requires Palau to submit economic development plans every 5 years, as well as annual reports on, among other things, its implementation of these plans. The agreement also requires the U.S and Palau governments to hold annual economic consultations to review Palau's progress toward self-sufficiency.

Additionally, the compact's subsidiary trust fund agreement requires the U.S. and Palau governments to consult regarding Palau's trust fund every 5 years. The Department of the Interior's (Interior) Office of Insular Affairs (OIA) has primary responsibility for monitoring and coordinating all U.S. assistance to Palau, and the Department of State (State) is responsible for government-to-government relations.

Direct assistance provided under title two of the compact is due to expire on September 30, 2009. At that time, Palau's annual withdrawals from its trust fund can increase from $5 million to $15 million.[4] The compact's federal programs and services agreement will, unless renewed or extended, also expire on September 30, 2009, ending the provision to Palau of three federal services—postal, weather, and aviation. The compact mandates that the governments of the United States and Palau review the terms of the compact and its related agreements in 2009 and that any modifications be made by mutual agreement.

You asked us to examine (1) the provision of compact and other U.S. assistance to Palau in 1995-2009, (2) Palau's and U.S. agencies' efforts to provide accountability over Palau's use of federal funds in 1995-2006, and (3) Palau's prospects for achieving economic self-sufficiency. In addition, we provide information on amendments made to the United States' compacts with the Federated States of Micronesia (FSM) and the Republic of the Marshall Islands (RMI) in 2003 and the relevancy of these amendments for Palau (see app. II).

To address our objectives, we reviewed Palau's compact annual reports, Palau's financial statements and internal control reports for 1995-2006, compact road project documentation, and economic studies. We interviewed officials from Interior; State; and the Departments of Agriculture (USDA), Defense (DOD), Education (Education), Health and Human Services (HHS), Homeland Security, Labor, and Transportation (DOT). In addition, we interviewed officials from the Federal Aviation Administration (FAA), the U.S. Postal Service (USPS), the National Weather Service (NWS)[5] and the U.S. Army Corps of Engineers (USACE), as well as economic experts from the International Monetary Fund (IMF) and the Asian Development Bank (ADB). In Palau, we interviewed government officials from a range of ministries, including the ministries of Finance, Health, Education, and Resources and Development, and the Office of the Public Auditor. We also met with private sector representatives and nongovernmental organizations in Palau, and we spoke with Palau's external auditor. We inspected the compact road and viewed infrastructure improvements to Palau's airport funded by FAA's Airport Improvement Program. We conducted this performance audit from October 2007 to June 2008 in accordance with generally accepted government auditing standards. Those standards require that we plan and perform the audit to obtain sufficient, appropriate evidence to provide a reasonable basis for our findings and conclusions based on our audit objectives. We believe that the evidence obtained provides a reasonable basis for our findings and conclusions based on our audit objectives. Appendix I provides more details on our objectives, scope, and methodology.

RESULTS IN BRIEF

U.S. aid to Palau in 1995-2009—compact direct assistance,[6] compact federal services, compact road construction, and discretionary federal programs—is expected to exceed $852 million.[7] Compact direct assistance, providing general budgetary support for Palau's government operations, will account for $411 million, or 48 percent of the assistance provided. Compact federal services—postal, weather, and aviation—will account for about $25 million, or 3 percent of the assistance, and compact road construction accounted for $149 million, or 17 percent of the assistance. Palau's receipt of discretionary federal program assistance will account for another $267 million, or 31 percent of the total assistance provided. For 1995-2006, five U.S. agencies—Education, HHS, Interior, DOD, and DOT—contributed the majority of discretionary federal program assistance to Palau.

Despite limited capacity to address persistent internal control weaknesses, Palau made progress in providing financial accountability and met most of the compact's and related agreements' accountability requirements; however, OIA provided limited monitoring of Palau's accountability for compact assistance. Palau's single audit reports for 1995-2006 show that it made progress in financial accountability by improving its timeliness in submitting the audit reports and improving the reliability of its financial statements. At the same time, the reports show persistent weaknesses in Palau's internal controls over financial reporting; the reports also indicate that Palau has not complied with all federal award requirements and show persistent weaknesses in Palau's internal control over compliance with these requirements. Although Palau has developed plans to correct these weaknesses, Palau's controller and Palau's external auditor said that limited capacity in financial accounting resources and expertise limits Palau's ability to execute these plans in a timely way. These weaknesses put Palau at risk of being unable to sustain its improvements in financial accountability and to operate a major federal program within applicable requirements. Palau met the majority of the compact's and related agreements' accountability requirements, such as submitting annual reports and economic development plans. OIA and

State officials, as well as officials from the government of Palau, reported that they participated in the economic consultations required by the fiscal procedures agreement but that the meetings were not held annually. Moreover, U.S. and Palau officials acknowledged that the required trust fund consultations were not held at all. According to OIA officials, OIA uses Palau's single audit results and compact annual reports to monitor Palau's use of compact funds but views its oversight role as limited.

Palau's prospects for economic self-sufficiency depend on four key factors: levels of continued U.S. assistance, the availability and value of trust fund withdrawals, fiscal reform to reduce Palau's dependence on these withdrawals, and private sector growth through an improved business environment.

- **U.S. assistance.** Given the $10 million scheduled increase in Palau's annual trust fund withdrawals in 2010, the expiration of $13.3 million in U.S. compact direct assistance at the end of 2009 will likely cause a net decline of less than 4 percent in Palau's national government revenues. However, potential increases or reductions in future levels of discretionary federal programs—estimated at $11.9 million in 2009— could have a significant fiscal impact. In addition, unless the federal programs and services agreement is extended by the U.S. and Palau governments, Palau will lose postal, weather, and aviation services that are estimated to cost U.S. agencies almost $1.6 million in 2009.

- **Trust fund withdrawals.** A compounded annual return of at least 8.1 percent will allow Palau to withdraw $15 million per year from its trust fund for the planned 35 years. From 1995 through March 2008, the Palau trust fund earned a compounded return of 9 percent.[8] However, market volatility makes it possible that the trust fund will be depleted after 2016 even with a favorable long-term average rate of earnings. In addition, future inflation will cause the withdrawals to lose value over time.

- **Fiscal reform.** To decrease its long-term reliance on trust fund financing, Palau will require fiscal reforms aimed at closing the gap between its revenues and expenditures. Specifically, experts suggest that Palau improve its tax income by addressing the problem of weak administration and an inefficient income and business tax structure and reduce its expenditures through lowering the public sector wage bill.

- **Private sector growth.** To promote private sector growth, Palau will need to improve its business environment. Currently, restrictive foreign investment regulations and practices, deficient financial oversight, inadequate access to land, and an inability to attract skilled workers raise private sector costs and weaken investment incentives.

To improve Palau's ability to sustain its improvements in financial reporting and address its internal control weaknesses, we recommend that the Secretary of the Interior direct the Office of Insular Affairs to formally consult with the government of Palau regarding Palau's financial management challenges and target future technical assistance toward building Palau's financial management capacity.

We provided a draft of this report to the Secretary of the Interior, the Secretary of State, and the government of Palau. The Department of the Interior agreed with our report and recommendation and said that it had begun making plans to implement the recommendation. The government of Palau also agreed with our report and recommendation. The Department of State did not comment on the report. In addition, we received technical comments from USDA, Education, and Homeland Security, as well as FAA, NWS, USPS, and the USACE.

BACKGROUND

U.S. relations with Micronesia began during World War II, when the United States ended Japanese occupation of the region. In 1947, the United Nations assigned the United States administering authority over the Trust Territory of the Pacific Islands, which included Palau and other Micronesian island districts. During its administration of the trust territory, the United States aided these islands by, among other things, building roads, hospitals, and schools; extending eligibility for U.S. federal programs; and supporting government operations. The trustees eventually sought various forms of independence and today comprise four island jurisdictions: the Commonwealth of the Northern Mariana Islands, an insular area under the sovereignty of the United States, and three Freely Associated States—the Federated States of Micronesia (FSM), the Republic of the Marshall Islands (RMI), and the Republic of Palau.[9] Palau adopted its own constitution in 1981, and the governments of the United States and Palau concluded a Compact of Free Association in 1986, similar to compacts that the United States had entered into with the FSM and the RMI. The compact entered into force on October 1, 1994, concluding Palau's transition from trusteeship to independence. As a sovereign nation, Palau conducts its own foreign relations. Palau is a member of the United Nations and has bilateral relations with more than 40 countries, including the United States and Japan, as well as the European Union. Palau also has diplomatic relations with Taiwan.

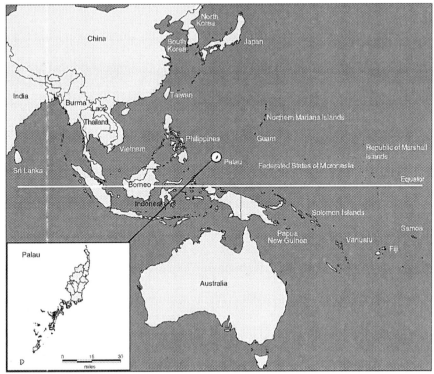

Source: GAO, Map Resources (map).

Figure 1. Location and Map of Palau.

Palau's territory of about 190 square miles includes 8 main islands and more than 250 smaller islands. As the westernmost cluster of the Caroline Islands in the North Pacific Ocean, Palau is located approximately 500 miles southeast of the Philippines (see figure 1). Roughly 20,000 people live in Palau, although more than one-quarter of the population is non-Palauan. The majority of the population lives in the single urban center, Koror, although the capital was officially moved in 2006 to Meleokeok, on Babeldaob, Palau's largest island. Meleokeok is the seat of Palau's national government, which has an executive branch, a legislative branch, and a judicial branch. The country is divided into 16 states, each with its own governor and legislature.

2000-2006 Average Expenditure by Type

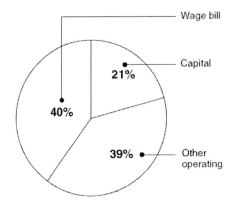

2006 Expenditure Level

	Dollars in millions ($)	Percentage of GDP (%)
Capital	22.7	15
Wage bill	33.2	22
Other operating	33.4	22
Total	89.3	58

2000-2006 Average Revenue by Source

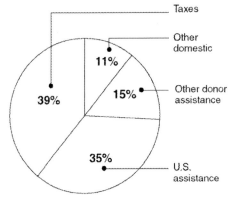

2006 Revenue Level

	Dollars in millions ($)	Percentage of GDP (%)
U.S. assistance	31.5	20
Other donor assistance	12.8	8
Taxes	29.4	19
Other domestic	9.6	6
Total	83.3	54

Source: GAO estimates based on Palau's single audit reports.

Notes:

GDP = gross domestic product.

Figures and tables exclude: (a) component units, such as the Palau Community College; (b) in-kind foreign assistance, such as compact federal services; and (c) annual net financing, such as Palau's $5 million trust fund withdrawal from 2002-2006, to pay for the gap between revenues and expenditures. Net financing is excluded as a revenue source given that the trust fund was designed to provide Palau with financing only until 2044, in addition to the market volatility associated with investment earnings.

"Other operating" expenditures include those for goods and services and "Other domestic" revenues include fees and charges, licenses, permits, and other direct revenues.

All years cited are fiscal years (Oct. 1-Sept. 30). All dollar amounts are in current (i.e., nominal) dollars.

Figure 2. Palau National Government Expenditures and Revenues.

Palau's economy is heavily dependent on its tourism sector and substantial foreign aid from the United States, Japan, and Taiwan. Since 1994, Palau's economy has grown at a real annual average of 3 percent; in 2006, Palau's gross domestic product (GDP) was about $154 million and its GDP per capita was about $7,500.[10] International visitor arrivals—more than 82,000 in 2006— contributed about $97 million to the economy. Similar to many small island economies, Palau also receives significant foreign aid, which finances a large public sector. In 2006, Palau's national government expenditures were $89 million, equivalent to 58 percent of its GDP, and the United States and other donors provided grants totaling $44 million, equivalent to 28 percent of Palau's GDP (see figure 2).[11] While 2006 national government expenditures exceeded total revenues, Palau also has access to financing through interest earned on government assets and allowed annual withdrawals on the compact-provided trust fund. Palau's government employs about one-third of all workers, and the national government wage bill constituted an average 40 percent of its total expenditures from 2000 to 2006. Palau's private sector relies heavily on foreign workers, mostly from the Philippines; since 1994, foreign workers[12] have grown to account for half of Palau's total labor force. Because many of these foreign workers send wage income back to their home nations, the annual net outflow of remittances from Palau equaled an estimated 5.5 percent of its 2005 GDP. (For further statistics on Palau's economy and assistance level as it compares to other compact nations, see app. III.)

Compact of Free Association

The Compact of Free Association between Palau and the United States became effective on October 1, 1994,[13] with the U.S. interest of promoting Palau's self-sufficiency and economic advancement. It also established certain national security objectives for Palau and the United States. The compact requires the United States to provide a 15-year term[14] of direct assistance and to set up a trust fund with the goal of producing an annual distribution of $15 million for 35 years, starting in 2010. The compact also includes certain security and defense provisions between the two countries, which are binding until 2044 unless amended by mutual consent. Other provisions of the compact continue in perpetuity unless mutually terminated by the two countries or individually by Palau or the United States. The compact mandates that the U.S. and Palau governments formally review the terms of the compact and its related agreements on the 15th, 30th, and 40th anniversaries of the effective date of the compact and mutually agree to any alterations. The first mandated review will take place in 2009.

Table 1. Key Provisions of the Palau Compact of Free Association and Related Subsidiary Agreements

Compact section	Description of key provisions
Title one: Government Relations	*Sovereignty*
	Establishes Palau as a self-governing nation with the capacity to conduct its own foreign affairs.
	Immigration privileges
	Provides Palauan citizens with certain immigration privileges, such as the rights to work and live in the United States indefinitely and to enter the United States without a visa or passport.
Title two: Economic Relations	*Compact direct assistance*
	15-year term of budgetary support for Palau, including direct assistance for current account operations and maintenance, and for specific needs such as energy production, capital improvement projects, health, and education.
	Requires the United States to set up a trust fund for Palau.
	This assistance expires in 2009.
	Compact road
	Requires the United States to build a road system for Palau (the "compact road").
	Compact federal services
	Requires the United States to make available certain federal services and related programs to Palau, such as postal, weather, and aviation services.
	The compact federal programs and services agreement—establishing the legal status of programs and related services, federal agencies, U.S. contractors, and personnel of U.S. agencies implementing both compact federal services and discretionary federal programs in Palau—expires in 2009.
	Accountability of compact funds
	Requires Palau to report annually on its use of compact funds.
	Requires the U.S. government, in consultation with Palau, to implement procedures for periodic audit of all grants and other assistance.

Compact section	Description of key provisions
Title three: Security and Defense Relations	Establishes that the United States has full authority and responsibility for security and defense matters in or relating to Palau.
	Forecloses Palau to the military of any other nation except the United States.
	The United States may establish defense sites in Palau and has certain military operating rights.
	Security provisions specified in the subsidiary status of force agreement[a] are binding until 2044, 50 years from the effective date of the compact, or until the termination of title three of the compact, whichever is longer.
Title four: General Provisions	Establishes general provisions regarding approval and effective date of the compact, conference and dispute resolution procedures, amendment and review requirements, and compact termination procedures.

Source: GAO analysis of the Compact of Free Association.

Note: The compact's subsidiary agreements relate to specific titles of the compact; in many cases, they contain implementing details of compact provisions.

[a]*Status of Forces Agreement Concluded Pursuant to Section 323 of the Compact of Free Association.*

Other U.S. Assistance to Palau

In addition to the U.S. assistance provided under the terms of the compact, U.S. agencies—Education, HHS, and Interior, among others—extend discretionary federal programs to Palau as authorized by U.S. legislation, and with funding appropriated by Congress for the programs. The federal programs and services agreement—which establishes the legal status of programs and related services, federal agencies, U.S. contractors, and personnel of U.S. agencies implementing both compact federal services and discretionary programs in Palau—expires in 2009.

Key Compact and Related Agreements Accountability Requirements

The compact's fiscal procedures agreement states that the U.S. government has the authority and responsibility to audit all compact funds[15] and requires Palau to submit audit reports each year on its use of compact funding, within the meaning of the Single Audit Act.[16] Single audit reports provide key information about Palau's financial management and reporting and are an important control used by federal agencies for overseeing and monitoring the use of federal grants.[17] These reports are due at the end of the third quarter following the end of the fiscal year under review. Interior is designated as the cognizant agency with respect to Palau's single audits;[18] OIA carries out the responsibilities associated with that designation. Interior's Office of the Inspector General (OIG) also has audit oversight responsibilities for federal funds in Palau. In addition, Palau's Office of the Public Auditor has authority to review the government of Palau's use of U.S. federal grant funds.[19]

In addition, the compact and related agreements require the Palau and U.S. governments to meet other reporting and consultation requirements to provide accountability over the use of compact funds.[20] An executive order regarding the management of the compact assigns Interior responsibility for monitoring and coordinating assistance provided under the compact and assigns State responsibility for government-to-government relations.[21]

- **Economic development plans.** Palau must submit an overall economic development plan to the U.S. government every 5 years, identifying the planned annual expenditure of compact assistance.[22] The U.S. government is required to review each plan in order to ascertain compliance and consistency with the requirements of the compact, to assist the government of Palau in identifying and evaluating appropriate goals and objectives, and to determine what U.S. government assistance might be made available to assist Palau in implementing the plan.
- **Annual reports.** Palau must submit an annual report to the U.S. government each year describing Palau's economic activities and progress in the previous year. The annual reports are required to describe Palau's implementation of its overall economic development plan and must include specific information on the use of compact funds and comprehensive information on Palau's trust fund.
- **Annual economic consultations.**[23] The U.S. and Palau governments must consult annually regarding the substance of Palau's annual reports. Specific topics to be discussed include all matters covered in the annual reports, Palau's expenditure of compact funding, and recommendations for issues to be addressed in future annual reports.
- **Trust fund consultations.** Beginning in 2000, the U.S. and Palau governments must consult every 5 years to discuss the performance of the trust fund and to evaluate the relationship between the performance of the

trust fund and the condition of Palau's operating expenditures. The two governments are required to take mutually-agreed upon action to resolve any issues identified.

U.S. ASSISTANCE TO PALAU IN 1995–2009 IS PROJECTED AT MORE THAN $852 MILLION

The United States' cost of providing assistance to Palau in 1995-2009 is projected to exceed $852 million. This assistance consists of compact direct assistance, compact federal services, compact road construction, and discretionary federal programs. The first three forms of assistance—compact direct assistance, compact federal services, and compact road construction—are mandated by the compact and represent approximately 48 percent, 3 percent, and 17 percent, respectively, of total projected U.S. assistance for 1995-2009. U.S. agencies provide the remaining 31 percent of total assistance through discretionary federal programs[24] (see figure 3).

Compact Direct Assistance

Compact direct assistance accounts for roughly half of projected U.S. assistance to Palau in 1995-2009, amounting to more than $411 million.[25] This assistance flows as a direct transfer payment to the government of Palau. The compact specifies general purposes for these funds but gives the Palau government broad discretion regarding the use of these funds.[26] Some direct assistance is provided annually for a period of 15 years from the effective date of the compact (i.e., 1995-2009). However, more than half of the direct assistance was provided in the first 3 years of the compact (see app. VII), allowing Palau to invest some of these funds to generate additional income. All compact direct assistance will terminate in 2009. Table 2 details the compact's provisions for direct assistance.

Palau reported the following uses of compact direct assistance in 1995-2006:

- More than one-quarter of direct assistance was provided to Palau under compact section 211(a) as annual budgetary support and used for general government operations. According to its compact annual reports, Palau distributed its 211(a) funds for uses such as supporting its executive, legislative, and judicial branches; independent agencies; and in block grants to states. In 2006, for example, Palau allocated $4 million to its executive branch; $1 million to its independent agencies, which includes its Office of the Public Auditor and Office of the Special Prosecutor; and $1 million to other agencies and programs, which include components such as its Coral Reef Center.

Dollars in millions

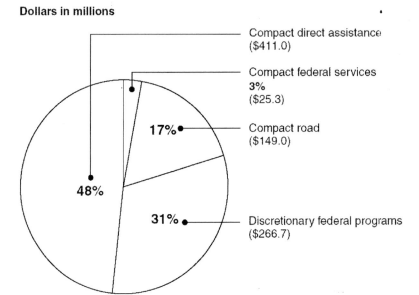

Source: GAO analysis.

Notes:

Figure shows funding for fiscal years (Oct. 1-Sept. 30). All dollar amounts are in current (i.e., nominal) dollars.

GAO's calculations of direct compact assistance and the compact road are based on Interior's Office of Insular Affairs' actual and estimated payments to Palau for 1995-2009, as reported in its budget justification to Congress for 2009. Compact federal services are estimates of past and future expenditures by the NWS, USPS, and the FAA. The calculation of estimated discretionary federal programs is the sum of U.S. agency program expenditures as reported in single audits for 1995-2006 for the Palau national government and for 1997-2006 for the Palau Community Action Agency and the Palau Community College. GAO projected U.S. agency program expenditures for 2007-2009. To this, we added an estimated cost of DOD's Civic Action Teams for 1995-2009. Estimated and projected federal program expenditures do not include the value of U.S. loans to Palau. For more details, see app. I.

Figure 3. U.S. Assistance to Palau 1995–2009 (projected).

Table 2. Compact Direct Assistance Provisions and Amounts, 1995–2009

Compact section	Description	Amount provided 1995–2009 (projected)
211(a)	*Current account operations and maintenance* $12 million annually for 10 years (1995-2004) and $11 million annually for the next 5 years (2005-2009). Beginning in 1999, $5 million of this amount shall come from the trust fund set up in 211(f).	$120 million
211(b)	*Energy production self-sufficiency* $2 million annually for 14 years (1995-2008).	$28 million
211(c)	*Communications* $150,000 annually for 15 years (1995-2009) for current account operations and maintenance of communications systems plus a sum of $1.5 million in 1995 for acquiring communications hardware or for another operating or capital account activity as Palau selects.	$3.75 million
211(d)	*Maritime zone surveillance and enforcement, health programs, and postsecondary scholarship fund* $631,000 annually for 15 years (1995-2009).	$9.5 million
211(e)	*Maritime zone surveillance and enforcement start-up activities* One-time contribution of $666,800.	$0.7 million
211(f)	*Trust fund* $66 million in 1995 plus $4 million in 1997.	$70 million
212(b)	*Capital account purposes* One-time contribution of $36 million in 1995.	$36 million
213	*Defense use impact fund* One-time contribution of $5.5 million in 1995.	$5.5 million
215	*Inflation adjustment* Yearly adjustment of amounts provided in sections 211(a), 211(b), 211(c), and 212(b).	$98.9 million
221(b) and federal programs and services agreement	*Special block grants for health and education* $2 million annually for 15 years (1995-2009), $4.3 million in 1995, $2.9 million in 1996, and $1.5 million in 1997.	$38.7 million
Total direct assistance		**$411 million**

Source: GAO analysis of the Compact of Free Association and OIA budget justification 2009.

Note: All years cited are fiscal years (Oct. 1-Sept. 30). All dollar amounts are in current (i.e., nominal) dollars.

- The United States provided the entire $28 million of section 211(b) funds to Palau in 1995, when the compact went into effect,[27] enabling Palau to accrue investment earnings on the base sum. According to Palau's compact annual reports, the government used 211(b) funds on a range of projects to achieve energy self-sufficiency, such as paying off its debt on its central power station and improving power systems in outlying states. Palau reports that it achieved electrification for all of its 16 states by 1999; states receive electricity from one of Palau's two main power stations or from the island states' alternate sources.
- Palau used section 211(c) assistance primarily for public broadcasting operations and 211(d) and 211(e) funds for purposes such as patrol boat operations, education scholarships, and medical supplies.
- Section 211(f) of the compact required the United States to establish a trust fund for Palau with an initial investment of $70 million by the compact's third year. In accordance with terms of the trust fund agreement, since 1999, $5 million of annual 211(a) assistance has been available from the trust fund, although Palau did not begin taking this disbursement until 2002.
- As specified in section 212(b), Palau received $36 million in fiscal year 1995 for capital account purposes. Funding was spent for purposes such as improvements to Palau's water system and national roads; rehabilitation of a power plant and schools; and construction of a national gymnasium, four health dispensaries, and education facilities. Palau also passed some of this funding to state governments for state-directed capital improvement projects.
- Funding for section 211(a), as well as the assistance granted in sections 211(b), 211(c), and 212(b), was increased because of the inflation adjustment dictated in section 215.[28] Inflation adjustment for these four sections will account for an additional $99 million in assistance by 2009.
- In 1997-2006, the Palau national government transferred the $2 million provided annually under section 221(b) of the compact for health and education purposes to the Palau Community College for its operations.

Compact Federal Services

The compact provides for federal postal, weather, and aviation services in Palau at a level equivalent to the services provided the year before the compact was implemented.[29] The federal programs and services agreement describes the provisions of each of these services. This agreement remains in force for 15 years from the effective date of the compact; as a result, U.S. provision of these three federal services will expire in 2009 unless the agreement is renewed or extended. U.S. agencies providing these services—USPS, NWS, and FAA—incur costs in doing so, but in some cases, the United States receives a reciprocal benefit.

USPS conveys mail[30] between the United States and Palau and offers other services such as Priority Mail®, cash-on-delivery, and postal money orders. USPS charges U.S. domestic postal rates[31] for mail sent between the United States and Palau. The government of Palau retains the revenue from stamps purchased in Palau, while USPS retains revenue from stamps purchased in the United States. USPS officials said that the postage charged does not reflect the real cost of conveying mail to Palau, especially with rising transportation costs.[32] USPS is reimbursed by Interior for providing postal services to Palau; however, according to USPS officials, the amount reimbursed is less than the total cost of service. This loss is reduced by USPS's revenue collected on stamps for Palau-bound mail purchased in the United States. In addition to transporting mail, USPS provides technical assistance to Palau's postal service and has made several donations of used equipment, such as mail trucks.

NWS reimburses Palau for the cost of operating its weather station in Palau. The weather station in Palau performs upper air observations twice daily with a weather balloon as well as additional weather observations on request. The station and the equipment are maintained by Palauan staff, which includes two meteorologists whose professional training was sponsored by NWS. The weather forecasts produced by the weather station are essential to Palau's airport operations. The station's observations are important to NWS in helping to predict cyclones and other violent weather traveling eastward from Palau toward U.S. territories such as Guam.

Table 3.Compact Federal Services, 1995–2009

Federal service	U.S. agency providing service	Estimated expenditures by U.S. agency providing service 1995-2009 (projected)
Postal service	U.S. Postal Service	$12.3 million
Weather service	National Weather Service	$8.6 million
Aviation service	Federal Aviation Administration	$4.4 million
Total		**$25.3 million**

Source: GAO analysis of estimates provided by USPS, NWS, and FAA.

Note: All years cited are fiscal years (Oct. 1-Sept. 30). All dollar amounts are in current (i.e., nominal) dollars.

FAA provides aviation services[33] to Palau, including en-route air traffic control from the mainland United States, flight inspection of airport navigation aids, and technical assistance and training.

Compact Road

The compact required the United States to build a road system in Palau based on specifications mutually agreed with the government of Palau. Interior's OIA budgeted $149 million for the project. While the compact required the road to be completed by October 1, 2000, the project incurred several planning and construction delays and was not completed until October 1, 2007. When the road was completed, Palau accepted responsibility for its operation and maintenance. Palau has made efforts to maintain the road; however, both U.S. and Palau officials have concerns regarding Palau's ability to maintain the road in a condition that will allow for the desired economic development. See appendix V for more information on the compact road.

Discretionary Federal Programs

Discretionary federal programs are projected to contribute approximately $266.7 million, or 31 percent, of total U.S. assistance to Palau between 1995 and 2009. Discretionary federal programs, which include federal grants, in-kind services, and loans provided by U.S. agencies, assist Palau in areas such as education, health, infrastructure improvement, and telecommunications. In 1995-2006, more than 14 U.S. agencies provided Palau federal grants and other in-kind services worth approximately $203 million.[34] Five agencies contributed the majority of discretionary assistance to Palau (see figure 4). Most of the federal grants awarded to Palau go to the national government; two other recipients are the Palau Community College and the Palau Community Action Agency, a nonprofit organization. Palau's national government spent approximately $132 million, or 73.6 percent of the $180 million, of the federal grants awarded to these three entities in 1995-2006.

- The U.S. Department of Education provided federal grants to both the national government of Palau and to the Palau Community College, an accredited, postsecondary vocational and academic institution.[35] These grants provided funding for a number of education services, including special and adult education programs, teacher training and curriculum development, and postsecondary financial aid. For example, approximately 550 of the 600 students at the Palau Community College receive Pell Grants, which were worth approximately $2.2 million in 2006. Other programs extended to Palau include Education's TRIO programs: Upward Bound, Upward Bound Math and Science, and Talent Search.[36] In 2006, 110 students participated in the Upward Bound program, which was worth approximately $360,000.[37]

Dollars in millions

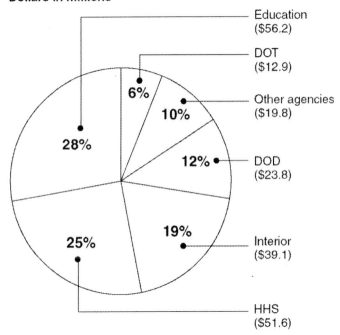

Source: GAO analysis.
Notes:
Figure shows expenditures for fiscal years (Oct. 1-Sept. 30). All dollar amounts are in current (i.e., nominal) dollars.
For all agencies, with the exception of DOD, our analysis used expenditure information reported in the single audits from the Palau national government, the Palau Community College, and the Palau Community Action Agency. GAO estimated DOD's expenditures for its Civic Action Team operating costs based on information provided by DOD officials. This figure does not include the value of other in-kind assistance provided by DOD or any other U.S. agency and it does not include the value of U.S. loans extended to Palau.

Figure 4. Top Five U.S. Agencies' Expenditures in Palau, 1995–2006.

- HHS supported Palau's Ministry of Health, particularly its Bureau of Public Health, with grant programs that fund a health clinic program, a family planning program, and immunization programs. HHS also provided federal grants to the Palau Community Action Agency, a private, nonprofit organization that runs the Head Start program in Palau.[38] According to Palau government officials, children are required to begin their education at 6 years of age; Head Start provides the primary early-childhood education and health program for children aged 3 to 5 years. The Palau Community Action Agency runs 13 Head Start education centers throughout Palau and receives funding for an enrollment of 509 children.

- Interior's OIA has provided a number of grants to Palau, including funding to cover the cost of Palau's single audit and technical assistance grants to provide training and support to finance and budget officials, the Public Auditor's office, and the Bureau of Lands and Survey. In addition, Interior has provided funds for emergency repairs to the national hospital and in support of infrastructure development through the Airport Improvement Program.

- DOD provided in-kind service assistance to Palau through its Civic Action Team (CAT). The CAT program consists of teams of 13 service men and women, primarily engineers, stationed in Palau for 6-month rotations. These teams provide assistance in the following four areas: (1) construction, (2) apprentice training, (3) community relations, and (4) a medical program.

- DOT provided a $26 million, 4-year grant (2003-2007) to Palau as part of the FAA's Airport Improvement Program. It enhanced the safety and capability of Palau's airport by rehabilitating the runway, purchasing fire fighting equipment, and installing perimeter security fencing.

- Ten other agencies extended federal grants to Palau in 1995- 2006. For example, the Department of Labor provided Workforce Investment Act funds to help finance job training and career development programs, and USDA extended forestry grant programs.

In addition to the federal grants and DOD CAT program costs enumerated in figure 4, U.S. agencies have provided a range of other assistance[39] to Palau to assist with maritime surveillance, disaster relief, education, and telecommunications. For example, DOD provided surveillance assistance to Palau to facilitate and enhance joint fisheries surveillance and enforcement. According to agency officials, DOD also has the authority to assist with natural disasters in

Palau. The Peace Corps has had a presence in Palau since 1966 and currently has 13 volunteers stationed there to assist in education programs primarily at public schools throughout the country.[40] The United States also has extended development loans to Palau.[41] USDA Rural Development provided subsidized loans to Palau through its utilities and housing programs. Through the utilities program, a \$39 million loan was provided in 1992 to the Palau National Communications Corporation to improve the telecommunications infrastructure in Palau. (For more information about this loan, see app. VI.) USDA's Rural Housing program provided 102 loans, worth over \$3.1 million, to individuals and families for the purchase or repair of their home in 1998-2007.

Table 4. Single Audit Act Report Submissions, 1995–2006

Year	Number of months late
1995	N/A[a]
1996	N/A[a]
1997	0
1998	2
1999	3
2000	29
2001	4
2002[b]	23
2003	11
2004	6
2005	0
2006	0

Sources: OMB Circular No. A-133, auditors' reports, Federal Audit Clearinghouse, and GAO analysis.

Note: All years cited are fiscal years (Oct. 1-Sept. 30).

[a] The Federal Audit Clearinghouse started receiving the Single Audit form (SF-FAC) in 1997; therefore, we are unable to determine the timeliness of the SF-FAC submission for 1995 and 1996. See GAO, *Single Audit: Update on the Implementation of the Single Audit Act Amendments of 1996*, GAO/AIMD-00-293 (Washington, D.C.: September 2000).

[b] The 2002 Single Audit report was reissued on May 23, 2005.

See appendix VI for more information regarding selected discretionary federal programs.

PALAU MADE PROGRESS IN ACCOUNTABILITY BUT HAS LIMITED CAPACITY TO ADDRESS INTERNAL CONTROL WEAKNESSES; INTERIOR'S OVERSIGHT HAS BEEN LIMITED

Palau's more recent single audit reports show that it made progress in financial accountability by improving its timeliness in submitting the audit reports. The recent single audit reports also show that Palau has improved the reliability of its financial statements. However, the reports show persistent weaknesses in Palau's internal control over financial reporting. Additionally, the reports indicate that Palau has not complied with all federal award requirements and has weaknesses in its internal control over compliance with federal award requirements. However, limited capacity in financial accounting resources and expertise hinders Palau's ability to address these weaknesses in a timely way. As a result, Palau is at risk of being unable to sustain its improvements in financial accountability and to operate a major federal program according to applicable requirements. Palau met the majority of the compact's and related agreements' reporting requirements for accountability over compact funds, but Palau and the U.S. government did not meet all of the consultation requirements. Interior's oversight of Palau's accountability for assistance provided under the compact was limited.

Palau's Single Audits Show Improved Financial Accountability but Also Persistent Internal Control Weaknesses that Palau Has Limited Capacity to Address

The Palau national government has improved its financial accountability in terms of the timeliness of its single audit report submissions. In addition, Palau's recent single audit reports show progress in improving the reliability of its financial statements. However, the reports also show persistent weaknesses in Palau's internal control over financial reporting. In addition, Palau's single audit reports show long-standing weaknesses in its internal control over compliance with laws and regulations governing federal awards. Although Palau has developed plans to correct its internal control weaknesses, its capacity to execute these plans in a timely manner is limited. As a result, Palau is at risk of being unable to sustain its improved financial accountability.

Palau's Timeliness in Submitting Single Audit Reports Has Improved

Palau's timeliness in submitting single audit reports has improved in recent years. Although Palau submitted its single audit reports for 1998-2004 after the established deadlines,[42] Palau submitted reports for 2005 and 2006 on time.[43] (See table 4.) Timely submission of single audit reports gives U.S. agencies current knowledge of the Palau government's ability to account for federal grant monies received and current knowledge of the government's internal control and compliance challenges.

Palau Has Improved Financial Statements' Reliability but Lacks Capacity to Address Internal Control Weaknesses

For 1995-2002, Palau received qualified audit opinions on its government's financial statements, indicating that significant issues prevented the auditor from concluding that the financial statements were reliable overall.[44] However, for 2003-2006, Palau's financial statements consistently received unqualified audit opinions, indicating that the auditor considered the statements reliable. (See table 5.)

Table 5. Financial Statement Audit Opinions for Palau, 1995–2006

Year	Opinion on financial statements
1995	Qualified
1996	Qualified
1997	Qualified
1998	Qualified
1999	Qualified
2000	Qualified
2001	Qualified
2002	Qualified
2003	Unqualified
2004	Unqualified
2005	Unqualified
2006	Unqualified

Source: Palau national government's single audit reports for 1995-2006.
Note: All years cited are fiscal years (Oct. 1-Sept. 30).

Despite the improved reliability of its financial statements, Palau has longstanding and significant weaknesses in its internal control over financial reporting.[45] Palau's 2006 single audit report cited a number of significant weaknesses in basic internal control that impact its financial reporting, many of which were cited in previous audit reports.[46] These weaknesses include, for example, nonresolution of differences in monthly bank reconciliations and a lack of policies and procedures for reconciling accounts receivable and prepayments.

Palau has developed corrective action plans to address these weaknesses, such as improving reconciliations to ensure proper entries and adjustments. Palau also is updating its financial reporting policies and procedures, which, according to officials from Palau's Ministry of Finance, date back to 1983. However, according to Palau's controller and Palau's current external auditor, Palau has inadequate staff and expertise to properly address its financial reporting weaknesses and make other necessary improvements in a timely manner. For example, Palau relies heavily on one individual to prepare its financial statements and has had difficulty in hiring a Chief of Finance and Accounting. As a result, Palau is at risk of being unable to sustain the improvements it has made in its financial accountability.

Palau Has Weaknesses in Its Compliance with Federal Award Requirements and Lacks Capacity to Address These Weaknesses

Since 1995, Palau's single audits have consistently received qualified opinions on its compliance with federal award requirements owing to long-standing and significant internal control weaknesses over its compliance with such requirements.[47] These weaknesses could adversely affect Palau's ability to operate a major federal program within the applicable requirements of laws, regulations, contracts, and grants. For example, in 2006, Palau's auditor cited noncompliance and internal control weaknesses in areas such as procurement, cash management, and equipment and real property management.[48] Many of the problems noted in the 2006 report were recurring. For instance, the weakness involving lack of effective controls to ensure that property is adequately safeguarded from loss, damage, or theft, had existed since 1988.[49]

Palau has developed corrective action plans to address the 2006 single audit findings regarding its compliance with, as well as its internal control over compliance with, federal grant requirements. For example, according to the 2006 report, Palau plans to strengthen internal controls over procurement and address its long-standing weaknesses related to adequately accounting for its equipment and real property.[50] However, Palau's limited staff and expertise hinder its ability to address the single audit report's findings in a timely manner.

Most Compact-related Reporting Requirements Were Met but Consultation Requirements Were Not, and Interior's Oversight Was Limited

Palau met the majority of the compact's and related agreements' reporting requirements. Palau and U.S. officials reported meeting some consultation requirements but in most cases did not document their compliance. In addition, Interior's OIA and OIG made efforts to assist or oversee Palau's accountability for compact funds; however, according to agency officials, OIA viewed its oversight role as limited and informal.

- **Economic development plans.** Palau prepared a two-volume economic development plan for 1995-1999. It updated this plan with an economic study for 2000-2005, which was completed by the Japan International Cooperation Agency. According to an official from Palau's Ministry of Finance, the next plan is expected to be completed at the end of 2008. An Interior official said that several U.S. agencies, including State and Interior, provided comments to Palau on its initial economic development plan.

- **Annual reports.** Palau completed the required annual reports and submitted them to the U.S. government. According to an Interior official, although the agency has reviewed the annual reports, Interior has not issued any formal written responses to Palau. As a result, there is no documentation regarding whether the U.S. government compared the actual use of the compact funds in the preceding year with the projected amount or whether the U.S. government agreed or disagreed that Palau used compact funds as set forth in its economic development plan.

- **Annual economic consultations.** Officials from the government of Palau, as well as OIA and State officials, told us that the U.S. and Palau governments held the required economic consultations.[51] However, the officials said that the meetings were informal and that they did not produce any written documentation, such as minutes, as a result of the meetings. State and OIA officials acknowledged that the meetings did not occur on an annual basis and that they usually occurred when other meetings between the two countries took place. An OIA official told us that the consultations usually lasted about a half-day. Although the compact does not require the Palau and U.S. governments to produce written documentation as a result of the consultations, the lack of documentation prevents any assessment of the meetings' effectiveness.

Furthermore, the lack of documentation makes it impossible to ascertain whether these informal consultations resulted in any recommendations, which the fiscal procedures agreement requires to be produced to the maximum extent possible.

- **Trust fund consultations.** Officials from the government of Palau and from OIA stated that trust fund consultations, required to occur at 5-year intervals, did not take place. Because the trust fund consultations did not take place, Palau may have lost the opportunity to discuss concerns about its trust fund with the United States. For example, officials in Palau told us that they interpreted the compact and related agreements as prohibiting trust fund managers from investing in anything other than U.S. securities. However, the trust fund agreement states that the United States government, in consultation with the government of Palau, shall consider designating other investment-grade instruments as qualified in order that the fund's performance objectives are met. If the trust fund consultations had taken place, the government of Palau could have raised this issue.

Interior's OIA and OIG reported efforts to assist or oversee Palau's accountability for federal funds. According to Interior officials, it has monitored Palau's progress in completing and issuing its single audit reports; used Palau's single audit and compact annual reports to monitor Palau's use of compact funds; worked with Palau to track single audit findings and resolve issues; and, considered Palau's requests to extend its single audit submission deadlines. In addition, according to Interior officials, OIA has provided general technical assistance funds to train Palau employees as well as funds to enhance Palau's financial management systems and processes. Interior officials also noted that Interior's OIG reviewed the single audit reports to determine whether they met applicable reporting standards and requirements.

However, an OIA official said that its oversight of compact funding has not been extensive, because compact assistance is given to Palau with the full faith and credit of the United States and because the compact gives Palau broad discretion in compact spending. In a 2006 memorandum, Interior's OIG criticized OIA for its minimal oversight and monitoring of Palau's compact funding. Although the memorandum did not contain recommendations, it suggested that OIA commit additional resources, such as a full-time staff member, to oversee accountability for compact funds and any other U.S. assistance provided to Palau.

PALAU'S PROSPECTS FOR ECONOMIC SELF-SUFFICIENCY DEPEND ON MULTIPLE FACTORS

Palau's prospects for long-term economic self-sufficiency depend on at least four factors: levels of continued U.S. assistance, the availability and value of trust fund withdrawals, fiscal reform to reduce Palau's long-term dependence on these withdrawals, and private sector growth through an improved business environment. Regarding continued U.S. assistance, given the scheduled increase in Palau's annual trust fund withdrawals in 2010, the expiration of compact direct assistance at the end of 2009 will likely cause a net decline of less than 4 percent in the Palau national government's revenues. Potential increases or reductions in the future levels of discretionary federal programs could have a significant fiscal impact. Moreover, unless the federal programs and services agreement is extended beyond 2009, Palau will lose postal, weather, and aviation services. Regarding the trust fund withdrawals, a compounded annual return of at least 8.1 percent will allow Palau to withdraw $15 million per year from its trust fund for the planned 35 years; however, market volatility makes it increasingly probable that the trust fund will be depleted after 2016, and inflation will cause the withdrawals to lose value over time. To decrease its reliance on trust fund financing, Palau will require fiscal reforms to close the gap between its revenues and expenditures. Regarding private sector growth, Palau will need to improve its business environment by addressing problems with its foreign investment climate; financial system; and land, labor, and commercial policies that presently discourage such growth.

Prospects for Economic Self-sufficiency Depend on Levels of Continuing U.S. Assistance

Palau's prospects for economic self-sufficiency depend in part on levels of continuing discretionary federal program assistance. We estimate that in 2009, the Palau national government's potential revenues—compact direct assistance, discretionary federal programs, other donor assistance, and domestic revenues[52]— will total about $87 million (see figure 5). Domestic revenues, at about $44 million in 2009, will have grown from about $30 million in 2000, based on the annual growth rate of 4.4 percent from 2000-2006. Other donor assistance, at about $18 million in 2009, will have grown from about $6 million in 2000, based on its annual growth rate of 17.4 percent from 2000-2006. In addition to potential revenues, Palau's government also will have access to financing through earned interest and annual withdrawals from the U.S. trust fund and other government assets. (For further fiscal information on Palau's national government, see app. III.)

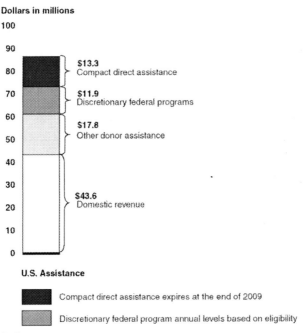

Dollars in millions

$13.3
Compact direct assistance

$11.9
Discretionary federal programs

$17.8
Other donor assistance

$43.6
Domestic revenue

U.S. Assistance

Compact direct assistance expires at the end of 2009

Discretionary federal program annual levels based on eligibility

Source: GAO analysis.

Notes:

Years cited are fiscal years (Oct. 1-Sept. 30). All dollar amounts are in current (i.e., nominal) dollars.

Domestic revenue includes taxes, fees and charges, licenses and permits, and other direct revenues and excludes net investment earnings. Total revenues exclude revenues for component units and in-kind assistance, such as compact federal services. In addition to revenues, Palau will have access to financing, including a $5 million annual trust fund withdrawal. Further fiscal information is provided in app. III.

To estimate potential 2009 domestic revenue and the level of other donor assistance, we reviewed Palau single audit data for 2000-2006 and Palau budgets for 2007 and 2008 and applied the average annual growth rate from 2000-2008.

Discretionary federal programs exclude the value of DOD's Civic Action Team program that is provided in kind. To estimate potential 2009 discretionary federal program levels, we reviewed Palau budget data for 2008 and assumed the same level of federal programs would be provided in 2009, adjusted for inflation.

The 2009 level of compact direct assistance is based on U.S. agency budget data.

Figure 5. Palau National Government's Potential Revenues in 2009.

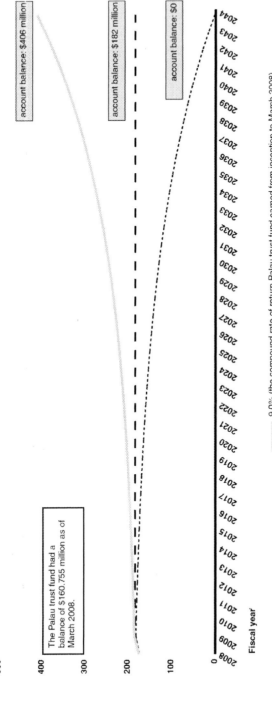

Palau Trust Fund Balance (in millions)

The Palau trust fund had a balance of $160.755 million as of March 2008.

account balance: $406 million

account balance: $182 million

account balance: $0

Fiscal year

— 9.0% (the compound rate of return Palau trust fund earned from inception to March 2008)
– – 8.6% (rate of return needed to grow the trust fund in perpetuity)
· · · · · 8.1% (rate of return needed to sustain the trust fund for 35 years)

Source: GAO analysis.

Note: Years shown are fiscal years (Oct. 1-Sept. 30). All return rates are net of fees and commissions.

Figure 6. Palau's Trust Fund Account Balance with Three Rates of Return.

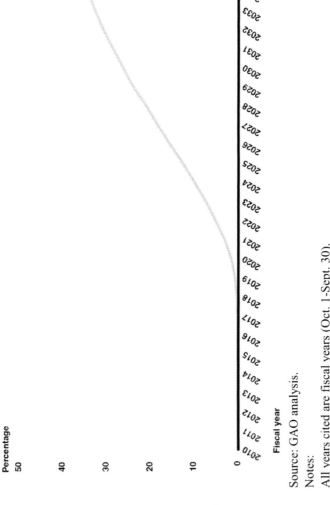

Percentage

50

40

30

20

10

0

Fiscal year

Source: GAO analysis.

Notes:

All years cited are fiscal years (Oct. 1-Sept. 30).

This chart depicts results from 10,000 trial runs. For each run, the returns of each of the asset classes are randomly drawn from a distribution based on the historical returns (1970-2007). The account balances and the amount of disbursements from the trust fund are then calculated based on the returns. The probability of not being able to disburse $15 million is then generated from a distribution of 10,000 disbursements each year.

Figure 7. Probability That Palau Trust Fund Will Be Depleted Given Market Volatility, 2010–2044.

Although the expiration of compact direct assistance at the end of 2009 will reduce the national government's revenues by about $13.3 million, Palau will gain access to an additional $10 million in annual financing when its yearly trust fund withdrawals increase in 2010 from $5 million to $15 million. As a result, the net fiscal impact of expiring compact direct assistance will be about $3.3 million annually, or less than 4 percent of the national government's revenues in 2009. However, levels of other forms of U.S. assistance after 2009 will impact Palau's fiscal condition:

- **Discretionary federal programs.** Since most federal programs operating in Palau are discretionary, they supply varied levels of annual assistance. For example, discretionary federal program assistance to the national government grew from $7.3 million in 2000 to $18.8 million in 2006, but is expected to fall to $11.3 million in 2008.[53] Although discretionary federal program funding in 2009 could total almost $12 million, or 14 percent of the national government revenues, future program funding will depend on Palau's program eligibility status and the availability of appropriations. Palau's eligibility for some federal programs may expire, absent affirmative action by Congress. In addition, the expiration of the compact's federal programs and services agreement in 2009 may impact U.S. agencies' implementation of discretionary federal programs in Palau. However, U.S. agency officials we interviewed expressed uncertainty about the extent of any such impact.

- **Compact federal services.** If compact federal services expire as scheduled at the end of 2009, the Palau national government may seek to provide these services with its own revenues. For example, unless the federal programs and services agreement is renewed or extended, Palau will lose postal, weather, and aviation services that are estimated to cost U.S. agencies almost $1.6 million in 2009.

Prospects for Economic Self-sufficiency Depend on Availability and Value of Trust Fund Withdrawals

Palau's prospects for economic self-sufficiency also depend in part on the availability of the planned $15 million annual trust fund withdrawals and the value of those withdrawals over time. Palau will be able to withdraw $15 million per year from its trust fund for the planned 35 years—from 2010 through 2044— if the fund earns a compounded annual return of at least 8.1 percent.[54] To grow in perpetuity, the trust fund must earn a compounded return rate of 8.6 percent or higher. Both of these rates are lower than the 9 percent return that the trust fund has earned from its inception in 1995 through March 2008; however, forecasts of future returns are subject to considerable uncertainty. The historical rate of return for the asset classes held in the fund's portfolio differ depending on the time period considered. For example, the compounded rate of return was 8.1 percent for 1926-2007, 9.1 percent for 1970-2007, and 5.2 percent for 1998-2007.[55] If the trust fund continues to earn the 9 percent annual return it has earned thus far, or any rate equal to or greater than 8.6 percent, the trust fund will likely grow in perpetuity from its balance as of March 2008 (see figure 6).

However, market volatility adds uncertainty regarding the availability of the trust fund withdrawals. Despite its historical compounded annual return rate of 9 percent as of March 2008, the trust fund's annual investment returns have ranged from 24 percent in 1998 to negative 12 percent in 2002. Future returns to the Palau trust fund portfolio are uncertain. Even if the trust fund earns a favorable long-run return which could allow the fund to grow in perpetuity without market volatility,[56] a few consecutive years of poor stock market performance could lead to the depletion of the trust fund. Figure 7 illustrates results from our analysis with the assumption that future returns are drawn from distributions based on historical 1970-2007 returns of the asset classes in which Palau's trust fund is invested. Our analysis shows that the trust fund will be able to disburse $15 million per year through 2016 but is increasingly likely to be depleted after 2016. For example, by 2030, 20 years after the annual $15 million disbursement begins, the probability of the trust fund depletion is close to 26 percent; by 2044, 35 years after the $15 million disbursement begins, the probability reaches approximately 46 percent. Figure 7 illustrates results from our analysis based on the historical returns for 1970-2007 of the asset classes held in the Palau trust fund. (For a detailed discussion of our methodology and results, see app. IV.)

In addition, inflation will diminish the value of the annual trust fund withdrawals: because the withdrawals are not adjusted for inflation,[57] they will lose real value over time. We estimate that by 2044—the last year of planned trust fund assistance—the value of the annual withdrawal will have decreased by about half compared with its value in 2010.[58]

Prospects for Economic Self-Sufficiency Depend on Fiscal Reform

Palau's prospects for economic self-sufficiency depend in part on fiscal reform to reduce Palau's long-term dependence on trust fund withdrawals.

Government officials and IMF experts have defined fiscal sustainability for Palau after 2009 as having sufficient domestic revenues, such as tax and fee income, to pay for operating expenditures, such as those for wages, goods, and services.[59] Continued donor assistance could be used to pay for capital expenditures. In 2000-2006, domestic revenues provided an average of 50 percent of national government revenue, while operating expenditures accounted for an average of 79 percent of national government spending. Beginning in 2010, Palau will have access to the $15 million annual trust fund withdrawals to finance the gap between its revenues and expenditures. However, Palau's long-term fiscal sustainability relies on reduced dependence on the full trust fund withdrawal, given (a) the uncertainty of continued donor assistance for capital spending, (b) the declining real value of the annual withdrawal, and (c) the planned exhaustion of the trust fund in 2044, with risks for its earlier exhaustion due to market volatility.[60] According to economic experts, Palau officials, and the country's economic plans, implementation of tax and expenditure reforms will be needed to close the gap between Palau's revenues and expenditures, although full implementation of such reforms is expected to require 10 to 15 years.[61]

Tax revenues. In 2006, tax revenue provided about $30 million and was equivalent to 19 percent of GDP, a level broadly comparable to that of other Pacific island nations. However, IMF and Asian Development Bank (ADB) experts describe Palau's tax system as inefficient because of, among other problems, weak tax administration and ineffective tax policy:

- *Tax administration.* Tax compliance in Palau is low, and the government rarely collects assessed penalties and interest or exercises its authority to suspend or revoke business licenses. The IMF and ADB estimate that fewer than 50 percent of active taxpayers are fully compliant. For example, in a 2004-2005 review, the Palau Office of the Public Auditor found that Palau lost more than $7.5 million in uncollected taxes and penalties for just 15 businesses in 1998-2005.[62] Also, although the government conducts tax audits, it rarely closes noncompliant businesses and usually waives penalties and interest. For example, in 2007, the government settled with Palau Marine Industries Corporation to pay $1.25 million on a court-awarded total obligation of over $5.7 million for unpaid taxes from 1999 through 2004.[63] The IMF and ADB are working with Palau on a tax modernization project to improve Palau's tax administration and possibly establish a Large Taxpayer Unit to focus on Palau's largest taxpayers.

- *Tax policy.* Experts and officials stated that Palau's tax policy allows numerous and complicated exemptions, and the current system does not tax nonwage income, such as that from profits, investment, or property. Additionally, Palau taxes businesses on gross, rather than net, earnings. To address these problems, Palau has consulted with the IMF and ADB since the 1990s and began devising tax reform legislation in 1998. However, Palau authorities indicated an intention to focus initially on short-term measures, primarily addressing rates and exemptions, and pursue structural reform over the long term. Palau's 2007 Tax Reform Task Force suggested 19 short-term measures that it estimated could provide an additional $31 million in revenues. To date, 2 of the 19 measures—increasing the hotel room tax rate and fish export tax rate—have been implemented.

Expenditures. Economic experts and government officials also suggest that Palau could lower its operating expenditures, at around $67 million in 2006, by reducing the public sector wage bill:

- *Public sector wage bill.* Although Palau has slightly reduced nonwage operating expenditures since 2000, it has been less successful in reducing the wage bill. From 2000-2006, Palau's national government wage bill grew from 46 percent to 50 percent of its operating expenditures, with wage levels nearly twice those in the private sector. According to government officials, Palau instituted a freeze on public sector employment in 2001 that has not been observed, and recent public sector reclassification efforts will result in a further increase in wage expenditures.[64]

Palau's Prospects for Economic Self-sufficiency Depend on Improved Business Environment for Private Sector Growth

Palau's prospects for economic self-sufficiency depend in part on the growth of its economy through private sector expansion, which will require an improved business environment. Palau's strategy for expanding its private sector focuses primarily on pursuing environmentally sustainable growth by promoting high-end tourism and capitalizing on growth opportunities from the new compact road.[65] Officials, experts, and private sector representatives view the tourism sector as offering the most potential for growth. For example, the IMF estimates that every

2 percent increase in tourist arrivals creates a 1 percent increase in tourism-related employment and that more than a third of foreign direct investment occurs in this sector. Current Palau tourism strategies aim to capitalize on opportunities for high-end tourists[66] from Asia and from U.S. military bases on Guam. The marine and agricultural industries together provide less than 5 percent of GDP; however, Palau is pursuing opportunities in aquaculture and considering whether foreign fishing license fees could be raised. In all cases, private sector development is dependent on sustained exploitation of Palau's fragile environmental resources.[67]

However, according to Palau government officials, economic experts, and private sector representatives, problems related to Palau's foreign investment policies, financial systems, land ownership system, labor market, and commercial conditions create a costly business environment that discourages private sector growth:

- **Foreign investment policies.** Palau imposes stringent requirements on foreign investment, restricting foreign investment in certain activities and requiring all applications to be approved by its Foreign Investment Board. According to officials from the board and Palau's foreign investment regulations, foreign investment in allowed activities must meet a minimum of $500,000 or have a minimum 20 percent Palauan ownership. Private sector representatives indicated that the Foreign Investment Board has significant discretion and applies the law inconsistently. Both officials and private sector representatives reported that burdensome requirements have encouraged the establishment of front businesses, where foreign investors operate illegally through a Palauan partner.

- **Financial systems.** Palau's financial markets do not effectively finance investment but instead supply large amounts of consumer credit. Moreover, Palau's foreign banks are unable to accept land as collateral, and financial regulations remain weak.[68] According to the IMF, Palau's Financial Institutions Act allows for insufficient bank liquidity and does not sufficiently empower the government to supervise bank compliance. The recent failure of Pacific Savings Bank illustrates the impact of weak regulation.[69] In commenting on this report, officials from Palau's Financial Institutions Commission said that recent legislative amendments will allow the Commission to strengthen its supervision of Palau's banking industry.

- **Land ownership system.** Palau's system of land ownership prevents the effective use of land for development. Much of Palau's land is family owned and not officially registered. Palau's Land Court is working to ensure that all lands are registered. However, Bureau of Lands and Surveys officials were unable to locate reliable statistics on registrations and suggested that fewer than 3,000 of 17,000 existing parcels had been referred to the Court. Separately, Land Court officials suggested that about 4,100 parcels had been registered.

- **Labor market.** Private sector representatives indicated a lack of available skilled labor in Palau, and Palau government officials expressed concern about illegal importation of unskilled foreign workers. ADB reports emphasize that current labor laws discriminate against the import of skilled labor and that minimum wage laws for Palauan workers encourage importation of unskilled foreign labor through unlicensed recruiters. Palau's Department of Labor receives many grievances from the Philippines Embassy about treatment of unskilled workers, who are often paid less than $150 per month and lack health benefits.

- **Commercial conditions.** Experts describe Palau's commercial legal system as outdated and lacking laws for bankruptcy, sales, and consumer privacy protection. Additionally, private sector representatives complained that the government often delays payment of vendors for several years.[70] Officials and private sector representatives also emphasized that, owing to the small size of the population, government officials often engage in private sector activities that create commercial conflicts of interest. For example, according to these officials and representatives, government officials with interests in construction companies or banking often are unwilling to enforce environmental or financial regulations.

CONCLUSION

In 2009, the governments of the United States and Palau will formally review the terms of the compact and its related agreements. Compact and other U.S. assistance has contributed to several areas important to Palau's self-sufficiency and economic advancement. For example, Palau used U.S. assistance to support governmental operations, maintain needed services, develop infrastructure, and improve public health and education. Although compact direct assistance will expire in 2009, the provision of federal services—postal, weather, and aviation— may continue if the federal programs and services agreement is renewed or extended. Moreover, it is likely that some discretionary federal programs will continue, although the level of federal program funding depends on Palau's continued eligibility, which may require affirmative action by Congress in some cases. Interior's OIA will continue to be the cognizant agency for Palau for the remaining compact direct assistance and to review Palau's single audits as long as U.S. federal program funds are expended in Palau. Palau has made progress in financial accountability, improving the timeliness of single audit report submissions and the reliability of its financial statements. However, Palau's single audit reports show persistent weaknesses in Palau's internal controls over financial reporting and compliance with federal award requirements. At the same time, Palau has limited capacity to address these weaknesses in a timely manner. Unless Palau strengthens its financial accounting resources and expertise, its ability to sustain its recent progress in financial accountability and to operate a major federal program according to applicable requirements is at risk.

RECOMMENDATION FOR EXECUTIVE ACTION

To strengthen Palau's ability to provide accountability and meet applicable requirements for federal assistance, we recommend that the Secretary of the Interior direct the Office of Insular Affairs to (1) formally consult with the government of Palau regarding Palau's financial management challenges and (2) target future technical assistance toward building Palau's financial management capacity.

APPENDIX I. OBJECTIVES, SCOPE, AND METHODOLOGY

This report examines (1) the provision of compact and other U.S. assistance to Palau from 1995-2009,[71] (2) Palau's and U.S. agencies' efforts to provide accountability over Palau's use of federal funds in 1995-2006, and (3) Palau's prospects for achieving economic self-sufficiency.

To address our objectives, we reviewed the Compact of Free Association between Palau and the United States and subsidiary agreements related to the compact, Palau's compact annual reports for 1995-2006, Palau's single audit reports for 1995-2006,[72] Palau government budgets, economic studies, and documentation for the compact road project. We interviewed agency officials at the Department of the Interior's (Interior) Office of Insular Affairs (OIA) and Office of the Inspector General (OIG), and the Departments of State (State),

Agriculture (USDA), Defense (DOD), Education (Education), Health and Human Services (HHS), Homeland Security, Labor, and Transportation (DOT). We also interviewed officials from the U.S. Army Corps of Engineers (USACE), the Federal Aviation Administration (FAA), the U.S. Postal Service (USPS), and the National Weather Service (NWS), as well as economic experts from the International Monetary Fund (IMF) and the Asian Development Bank (ADB). We traveled to Palau where we conducted site visits and interviewed government officials from a range of ministries, including the ministries of Finance, Health, Education, and Resources and Development, and the Office of the Public Auditor. We also interviewed Palau's external auditor and met with representatives of the private sector and nongovernmental organizations in Palau. We inspected the compact road and viewed infrastructure improvements made to Palau's airport that were funded by FAA's Airport Improvement Program.

To identify compact and other types of U.S. assistance to Palau in 1995-2009, we reviewed the compact and its related agreements; Palau's compact annual reports; Palau government budgets; and single audit reports for the Palau national government, the Palau Community College, and the Palau Community Action Agency. We used OIA budget justifications to estimate compact direct assistance from 1995 to 2009, as well as the estimated U.S. cost for the compact road. We used information provided by agency officials at FAA, USPS, and NWS to estimate the cost of compact federal services. Because FAA's cost estimates included the costs of providing services to six airports in Micronesia, we divided this cost by six to calculate a general estimate of the costs associated with Palau's one airport. USPS provided us with cost estimates from 1995 through 2009. NWS provided us with cost estimates from 2004 through 2007; we averaged these 4 years of data to estimate the annual costs in 1995-2003 and 2008-2009. We used single audit information from the three primary grant recipients—the Palau national government, the Palau Community College, and the Palau Community Action Agency—to determine those entities' actual grant expenditures. We estimated the Palau national government's grant expenditures for 2007–2009 using its budgetary estimates for those years and we projected grant expenditures for the other two entities based on their 2006 actual expenditures, after adjusting for inflation. We used information provided by DOD officials to estimate the cost to the department of providing the Civic Action Team (CAT) to Palau in 1995-2009. To include personnel as well as operating expenses, we adjusted the CAT's 2007 personnel cost for inflation to provide a broad estimate for 1995-2009.

To assess Palau's and U.S. agencies' efforts to provide accountability over Palau's use of federal funds in 1995-2006, we reviewed the compact and its related agreements to identify specific monitoring and accountability responsibilities and assessed the extent to which the Palau and U.S. governments conducted those responsibilities. We met with State and OIA officials to learn about their monitoring and oversight activities. We interviewed Palau government officials to identify Palau's accountability measures over federal grant awards. We also interviewed Palau's external auditor to discuss Palau's single audit results, accountability mechanisms, and accountability challenges. We reviewed the Palau national government single audit reports for 1995-2006 as well as audit reports from Palau's Office of the Public Auditor. We determined the timeliness of submission of the single audit reports using the Federal Audit Clearinghouse's (FAC) "Form Date," which is the most recent date that the required SF-FAC data collection form was received by the FAC.[73] We noted that the form date is updated if revised SF-FACs for that same fiscal year are subsequently filed. Our review of the contents of the single audit reports' contents identified the auditors' opinions on the financial statements and on Palau's compliance with federal grant requirements, matters cited by the auditors in their qualified opinions, the numbers of material weaknesses and reportable conditions reported by the auditors, and the status of corrective actions. We did not independently assess the quality of the audits or the reliability of the audit-finding information. We analyzed the audit findings to determine whether they had recurred in successive single audits and were still occurring in the most recent audits, and we categorized the auditors' opinions on the financial statements and Palau's compliance with major federal programs. To determine oversight activities, we reviewed Interior's OIG memorandums issued in December 2005 and January 2006 on Palau, as well as the OIG's desk review of Palau's single audit reports for 2002-2006.

To analyze Palau's prospects for achieving economic self-sufficiency, we used the data we had developed concerning compact and other U.S. assistance to Palau, as well as Palau's national government budgetary information, to describe the role of U.S. financial assistance to the government of Palau. We reviewed Palau's compact annual reports, economic development plans, and data for sector employment and production levels. We also reviewed studies and interviewed officials from the U.S. and Palau governments, Palau's private sector, the IMF, and the ADB. As part of this analysis, we projected Palau's trust fund balance and likely disbursement. To do so, we built a simulation model with the following inputs: (1) the trust fund's balance at the beginning of the projection, (2) disbursement and inflation adjustment, (3) the trust fund balance projection equation, and (4) distribution of returns for the Monte Carlo simulation. The trust fund balance as of March 2008 is the beginning balance for the projection. We followed the disbursement schedule outlined in the compact and the trust fund agreement. We ran the Monte Carlo simulation to analyze the effect of market volatility on the trust fund balance and disbursement. We base our projection on historical returns and volatility; however, the actual return on the trust fund may be different.

To determine the challenges encountered in the planning, design, and construction of the compact road, and the challenges that remain for the maintenance of the compact road, we interviewed officials from OIA, State, USACE, and the Palau government; nongovernmental individuals, including the author of the maintenance plan for the compact road; and the representative of a contracting firm in Palau. In Palau, we inspected the entire compact road to identify any obvious problems with the road. We also visited other roads maintained by Palau and reviewed the equipment Palau uses to maintain roads. In addition, we reviewed reports, equipment inventories, contract documents, budgets, plans, manuals, guidance, Internet Web sites, court decisions, and laws relevant to the construction and maintenance of the compact road. We did not interview Daewoo Engineering and Construction Co., Ltd., the contractor for the compact road, due to ongoing litigation between the contractor and the United States. (See app. V for more information about the compact road.)

We conducted this performance audit from October 2007 to June 2008 in accordance with generally accepted government auditing standards. Those standards require that we plan and perform the audit to obtain sufficient, appropriate evidence to provide a reasonable basis for our findings and conclusions based on our audit objectives. We believe that the evidence obtained provides a reasonable basis for our findings and conclusions based on our audit objectives.

APPENDIX II. RELEVANCY OF AMENDMENTS MADE TO FSM AND RMI COMPACTS FOR PALAU COMPACT REVIEW

In 1986, the United States entered into a Compact of Free Association with the Federated States of Micronesia (FSM) and the Republic of the Marshall Islands (RMI).[74] The three countries renegotiated the compact in 2003 to provide an additional 20 years of economic assistance and to address defense and immigration issues.[75] The aims of the amended FSM and RMI compacts were to (1) continue economic assistance to the FSM and RMI while improving accountability and effectiveness; (2) continue the defense relationship between the United States and the FSM and the RMI including a 50-year lease extension of U.S. military access to Kwajalein Atoll in the RMI until 2066, with an option to extend for an additional 20 years to 2086; and (3) strengthen immigration provisions.[76] Some of these amendments may be relevant for the Palau compact review in 2009, but others may be less relevant due to the differences between Palau's compact and the FSM's and the RMI's compacts and Palau's performance under its compact.

FSM's and RMI's Renegotiated Compacts Continued Economic Assistance while Increasing Accountability Requirements

The FSM's and the RMI's amended compacts authorized additional economic assistance while increasing the accountability requirements for the two countries and the United States. The new authorized funding took the form of 20 years of annual grants, contributions to a newly established trust fund for each country, and an extension of federal services.[77] The amended compacts established additional accountability measures over the annual grant funds. For example, new authorized funding was targeted to priority areas such as health, education, the environment, and public infrastructure. Joint economic management committees were established for each country to more closely monitor and evaluate the FSM's and the RMI's progress, and annual reporting requirements were expanded. The United States and the FSM and the RMI jointly manage the two countries' trust funds. The amended compacts grant the United States the authority to withhold payments if either the FSM or the RMI fail to comply with grant terms and conditions or if they do not cooperate in U.S. investigations regarding use of compact funds.

Based on our interviews with U.S. government officials concerning Palau's compact review, it is unclear whether a new economic assistance package will be offered to Palau and, if it were offered, whether additional accountability measures would be sought. Moreover, the establishment of a trust fund for the FSM and the RMI is not relevant for Palau since Palau's initial compact included a trust fund. One issue that is relevant for Palau is the continuation of compact federal services—postal, weather, and aviation—which the United States provides to Palau. In our discussions with officials from USPS, NWS, and FAA, we were told that each agency would like to continue offering these services to Palau, although they may seek some minor changes to the services provided.

Defense Issues in the Amended FSM and RMI Compacts

The most significant defense-related change in the amended FSM and RMI compacts was the extension of U.S. military access to Kwajalein Atoll in the RMI. A few other expiring defense provisions were extended indefinitely in the amended compacts, such as the U.S. "defense veto" and the ability of FSM and RMI citizens to volunteer to serve in the U.S. military. In the amended FSM and RMI compacts, CATs were eliminated; instead, both countries were given access to humanitarian assistance programs that would emphasize health, education, and infrastructure projects that DOD would carry out. DOD officials told us that defense provisions in title three of the Palau compact do not expire until 2044. The provision of the CATs to Palau, which is provided for in the Palau compact's implementing legislation, continues indefinitely, although DOD officials told us the CAT program in Palau will continue until 2044.

Strengthened Immigration Provisions in the Amended FSM and RMI Compacts

Although the immigration provisions in the original FSM and RMI compact were not expiring, State targeted them as requiring change during the compact renegotiation process. The major change in the amended compacts is that FSM and RMI citizens were required to present a passport before being allowed to enter the United States, which the original compact did not require. Other changes to the immigration provisions tightened rules for the entry of naturalized citizens from the FSM and the RMI, amended provisions for adopted children, and amended conditions on admission for compact nonimmigrants.

State officials said that it would be desirable for immigration provisions of Palau's compact to be in line with the FSM and RMI compacts. This is one issue the U.S. government will look at in preparation for the 2009 compact review. Department of Homeland Security officials said that they would like citizens of Palau to be required to present passports for admission into the United States to aid officers in their inspection of Palauans' identity documents. Data requested from Homeland Security showed that some citizens of Palau enter the United States using identity documents other than a passport. However, the port director at the airport in Guam, the port of entry through which many Palauans enter the United States, did not cite specific concerns over this lack of a passport requirement. He said that the Palauans' ability to enter without a passport may cause some confusion at other ports where officers may be less familiar with

Palauan citizens' immigration privileges. In commenting on this report, officials from U.S. Customs and Border Protection stated that a passport requirement for citizens of Palau entering the United States would eliminate confusion at ports that typically do not see these individuals, and that it would be in alignment with the Western Hemisphere Travel Initiative requirements already in place. In addition, they stated that having a passport would facilitate Palauan citizens in obtaining a Social Security card, driver's license, or other government-issued identification cards that generally require a passport as a supporting document.

Supplemental Education Grant in the Amended FSM and RMI Compacts' Implementing Legislation

In addition to receiving compact grants, the FSM and the RMI are eligible for a Supplemental Education Grant. The amended compacts' implementing legislation authorized appropriations to the U.S. Secretary of Education on an annual basis beginning in 2005, to supplement the education grants under the amended compacts. The supplement grant is awarded in place of grant assistance formerly awarded to the countries under several U.S. education, health, and labor programs.

APPENDIX III. ECONOMIC INFORMATION FOR PALAU

This appendix provides fiscal and economic information for Palau's national government. Specifically, table 6 provides data on Palau's actual revenue and expenditures for 2000 to 2006 and estimated values for these items in 2009. In addition to its annual revenues, Palau has access to financing through net changes in its government assets. One key source of financing for Palau is interest earned on the compact-provided trust fund, as well as the permitted annual withdrawals from the fund. Given that this trust fund was designed to provide Palau with financing only until 2044, in addition to the market volatility associated with investment earnings, we have excluded net financing from the revenues illustrated in table 6. Instead, both net investments—defined as the net increase in the fair value of investments minus investment management fees—and annual trust fund withdrawals are provided as memo items in the table. For further information on 2006 fiscal and economic data for Palau, in comparison to the RMI and the FSM, see table 7.

Table 6. Palau's National Government Finances, 2000–2006

(Dollars in thousands)

	2000	2001	2002	2003	2004	2005	2006	Potential 2009[b]
Total revenue	$57,263	$58,925	$59,432	$65,551	$68,720	$73,717	$83,324	$86,606
Domestic revenue[a]	29,993	30,943	30,648	31,343	32,667	38,928	38,975	43,632
Tax income	24,398	25,648	24,097	24,723	26,130	30,085	29,376	35,599
U.S. assistance	20,908	21,091	21,481	21,962	26,320	21,225	31,525	25,185
Compact direct assistance	13,642	13,785	13,928	13,928	14,071	10,471	12,717	13,271
Discretionary federal programs[c]	7,266	7,306	7,553	8,034	12,249	10,754	18,808	11,914
Other donor assistance	6,362	6,891	7,303	12,246	9,733	13,564	12,824	17,789
Total expenditure	77,609	77,432	80,867	76,840	83,057	78,086	89,342	92,655
Operating expenditure[d]	65,108	62,071	59,829	61,495	63,030	64,450	66,614	67,616
Wages and salaries	29,990	30,573	31,405	32,759	31,910	32,309	33,242	34,580
Capital expenditures	12,501	15,361	21,038	15,345	20,027	13,636	22,728	25,039
Memo items								
Net investments[e]	16,863	−14,405	−3,439	18,191	10,748	18,273	9,866	—
U.S. trust fund withdrawal	0	0	5,000	5,000	5,000	5,000	5,000	5,000
Gross domestic product (GDP)	118,269	123,458	120,755	121,909	130,852	141,889	154,430	
U.S. cost of compact fed-eral services received[f]	1,742	1,742	1,745	1,749	1,584	1,623	1,678	1,595
Population (actual number)	18,766	19,092	19,409	19,717	20,016	20,303	20,579	
(Percentage of GDP (%))								
Total revenues	48%	48%	49%	54%	53%	52%	54%	
Domestic revenue	25%	25%	25%	26%	25%	2%7	25%	
Tax income	21%	21%	20%	20%	20%	21%	19%	

(Dollars in thousands)	2000	2001	2002	2003	2004	2005	2006	Potential 2009[b]
U.S. assistance	18%	17%	18%	18%	20%	15%	20%	
Compact direct assistance	12%	11%	12%	11%	11%	7%	8%	
Discretionary federal programs	6%	6%	6%	7%	9%	8%	12%	
Other donor assistance	5%	6%	6%	10%	7%	10%	8%	
Total expenditures	66%	63%	67%	63%	63%	55%	58%	
Operating expenditure	55%	50%	50%	50%	48%	45%	43%	
Wages and salaries	25%	25%	26%	27%	24%	23%	22%	
Capital expenditures	11%	12%	17%	13%	15%	10%	15%	
Memo items								
Net investments	14%	-12%	-3%	15%	8%	13%	6%	
U.S. trust fund withdrawal	0%	0%	4%	4%	4%	4%	3%	
U.S. cost of compact federal services received	1%	1%	1%	1%	1%	1%	1%	

Source: GAO estimates of Palau's single audit data.

Note: All data are for Palau's national government and exclude component units. Except for the U.S. cost of compact federal services received, population, and GDP, all data for 2000-2006 are based on Palau single audits. Years cited are fiscal years (Oct. 1-Sept. 30).

[a] Domestic revenue includes taxes, fees and charges, licenses and permits, and other direct revenue, and excludes the net change in the fair value of investments.

[b] To estimate potential 2009 domestic revenue and total expenditure, we reviewed Palau budgets for 2007 and 2008 and applied the average annual growth rate from 2000-2008. To estimate potential 2009 discretionary federal programs, we reviewed Palau's 2008 budget and assumed the same level of programs would be provided in 2009, adjusted for inflation. Similarly, we assumed the 2009 level of compact direct assistance and U.S. cost of compact federal services would be the inflation-adjusted value of those provided in 2008, based on U.S. agency budget data.

[c] Discretionary federal programs exclude those provided in kind, such as DOD's Civic Action Team program.

[d] Operating expenditure includes current expenditures and debt service and excludes investment management fees.

[e] Net investments include the net change in the fair value of investments minus investment management fees.

[f] The U.S. cost of compact federal services is based on U.S. agency budget data.

Table 7. Economic and Fiscal Data for the Three Compact Countries

	Palau	FSM	RMI
Economic statistics, FY 2006[a]			
Population	20,580	108,000	52,710
GDP per capita	$7,500	$2,190	$2,730
GDP (thousands)	$154,430	$236,900	$144,140
Foreign assistance (thousands)[b]	$44,350	$85,300	$58,500
Aid per capita	$2,160	$790	$1,110
International visitor arrivalsc	82,400	19,280	9,170
Remittances as a percentage of GDP[c]	-5.5%	2.5%	0.3%
Fiscal statistics, FY 2006[a]			
Government tax revenue as a percentage of GDP	19%	13%	17%
Government expenditure as percentage of GDP	58%	65%	65%
Total public sector employee earnings as percentage of GDP[d]	29%	33%	36%
Average public sector wage level ($US)	$11,900	$8,850	$11,330
Average private sector wage level ($US)	$6,380	$4,150	$5,070
Total U.S. assistance levels			
Total compact grant assistance provided under initial compact (billions)[e]	$0.6	$1.5	$0.7
Total compact grant assistance provided under amended compact (billions)[e]	—	$1.6	$1.1
Total U.S. trust fund contribution (millions)[f]	$70	$508	$271
Foreign assistance as percentage of national government revenue, 2000-2006 average[b]	50%	65%	64%
Average annual level of discretionary federal programs, 2002-2004 (millions)	$9	$45	$20

Source: Country compact reports, single audit data, and GAO estimates.

[a] All data is rounded to the nearest tenth. Fiscal data for Palau and the Republic of the Marshall Islands (RMI) are for the national government and for the Federated States of Micronesia (FSM) are for the consolidated government, including states. Years cited are fiscal years (Oct. 1-Sept. 30).

[b] Excludes in-kind foreign assistance.

[c] Data for remittances and RMI international visitor arrivals is for 2005.

[d] Total public sector employee earnings include data for the national, state, and local governments plus government agencies and component units in all three countries.

[e] The initial compact for Palau provided assistance for 15 years. The initial compact for the RMI and the FSM provided assistance for 17 years. Data for U.S. assistance provided under the compacts of free association exclude the value of compact federal services and discretionary federal programs, but include Kwajalein impact payments to the RMI and the U.S. compact road to Palau.

[f] The United States provided funding for a trust fund for Palau under the initial compact. The United States provided funding for trust funds for the FSM and the RMI under the amended compacts.

APPENDIX IV. TECHNICAL NOTES ON THE TRUST FUND SIMULATION MODEL

This appendix lists the key inputs that we used to simulate the trust fund income and balance for 2010 to 2044 and some key simulation results. The key inputs include: (1) the trust fund's balances at the beginning of the projection, (2) disbursement and inflation adjustment, (3) the trust fund balance projection equation, and (4) distribution of returns for the Monte Carlo simulation. Further, this appendix contains a table comparing the nominal and real compounded returns of a portfolio based on the Palau trust fund asset allocation during various time periods.

Key Simulation Inputs

1. *Trust Fund Balance at the Beginning of the Projection*
    Our projection starts with an account balance of $160.755 million as of March 2008. This balance is higher than the projection in the trust fund agreement, which shows the account balance at the end of 2008 to be $123 million (if disbursement happens at the beginning of the year) and $144 million (if disbursement happens at the end of the year). However, the projection table in the trust fund agreement contains errors. It shows the annual disbursement of $5 million starting from the effective date of the compact (1995), rather than from the fourth anniversary of the effective date of the compact (1999), as the compact calls for. Also, it did not include the additional $4 million U.S. contribution, which was made during the third year after the effective date of the compact (1997). We corrected these errors and then applied the return (12.5 percent) assumed in the trust fund agreement. We calculate that this would result in an end of 2008 balance of $268 million (if disbursement happens at the end of the year) or $259 million (if disbursement happens at the beginning of the year). These were both higher than the actual account balance as of March 2008. We also projected the balance at the end of 2009, which is $297 million (if disbursement happens at the end of the year) or $285 million (if disbursement happens at the beginning of the year); this is far less than the projected $390 million that Palau indicated should be in the trust fund during its March 2008 meeting with the United States.

2. *Disbursement and Inflation Adjustment*

Our projection assumes the disbursement is $15 million a year and the disbursement happens on a quarterly basis.[78] In their projections, both the IMF and the Palau trust fund investment advisor assumed that the disbursements are inflation adjusted. However, the compact does not specify that the trust fund disbursement be inflation adjusted.[79]

3. *Trust Fund Balance Projection Equation*

In order to project the trust fund balances beyond 2008, we used the following projection equation: $W\_t+1 = W\_t * (1+r\_t)*(1-F\_t) - AW\_t$, where

W_t+1 = value of the fund at the beginning of period t+1
W_t = value of the fund at the beginning of period t
r_t = the quarterly return in period t
AW_t = the quarterly withdrawal in period t
F_t = the fees as a percentage of account value the trust fund pays to its trustee, investment advisor, money managers, and lawyers, etc. (We assume the fees to be 1 percent of the account value annually.)

4. *Distribution of Returns for Monte Carlo Simulation*

We assume that future returns on the trust fund are randomly drawn from custom distributions, which are based on historical nominal returns for 1970-2007 of the various asset classes and the proportion of the asset in the investment strategy. The distributions for small company stocks, large company stocks, and U.S. Treasury bills are illustrated in table 8. The returns were published in Stocks, Bonds, Bills and Inflation (SBBI) 2008 Yearbook, by Ibbotson Associates.

MONTE CARLO SIMULATION

Our methodology for projecting trust fund income is based on a technique known as the Monte Carlo simulation. This problem-solving technique approximates the probability of certain outcomes by performing multiple trial runs, called simulations, using random variables. The simulations capture the volatility of market returns and reflect that volatility in the projection of the future earnings of the trust fund.

GAO has used the Monte Carlo simulation in past reports, including assessments of the FSM and the RMI trust funds, and it also has been used by the Congressional Budget Office in Social Security projections.

Table 8. Nominal Returns Distribution Based on Historical Data, 1970–2007

Small company stocks (%)			Large company stocks (%)			U.S. Treasury bills (%)		
Range		Probability	Range		Probability	Range		Probability
-30.9	- 21.56	2.70	-26.47	-22.1	2.70	1.02	1.2	2.70
-21.56	- 19.95	2.70	-22.1	-14.66	2.70	1.2	1.65	2.70
-19.95	- 17.43	2.70	-14.66	-11.88	2.70	1.65	2.9	2.70
-17.43	- 13.28	2.70	-11.88	-9.11	2.70	2.9	2.98	2.70
-13.28	-9.3	2.70	-9.11	-7.18	2.70	2.98	3.51	2.70
-9.3	-7.31	2.70	-7.18	-4.91	2.70	3.51	3.83	2.70
-7.31	-6.67	2.70	-4.91	-3.17	2.70	3.83	3.84	2.70
-6.67	-5.22	2.70	-3.17	1.31	2.70	3.84	3.9	2.70
-5.22	-3.59	2.70	1.31	4.01	2.70	3.9	4.39	2.70
-3.59	3.11	2.70	4.01	4.91	2.70	4.39	4.66	2.70
3.11	4.43	2.70	4.91	5.23	2.70	4.66	4.68	2.70
4.43	5.69	2.70	5.23	5.49	2.70	4.68	4.8	2.70
5.69	6.85	2.70	5.49	6.27	2.70	4.8	4.86	2.70
6.85	10.18	2.70	6.27	6.56	2.70	4.86	5.08	2.70
10.18	13.88	2.70	6.56	7.67	2.70	5.08	5.12	2.70
13.88	16.17	2.70	7.67	9.99	2.70	5.12	5.21	2.70
16.17	16.5	2.70	9.99	10.87	2.70	5.21	5.26	2.70
16.5	17.62	2.70	10.87	14.31	2.70	5.26	5.47	2.70
17.62	18.39	2.70	14.31	15.8	2.70	5.47	5.61	2.70
18.39	20.98	2.70	15.8	16.81	2.70	5.61	5.65	2.70
20.98	22.77	2.70	16.81	18.44	2.70	5.65	5.8	2.70
22.77	22.78	2.70	18.44	18.47	2.70	5.8	5.89	2.70
22.78	22.87	2.70	18.47	18.98	2.70	5.89	6.16	2.70
22.87	23.35	2.70	18.98	21.04	2.70	6.16	6.35	2.70
23.35	23.46	2.70	21.04	21.41	2.70	6.35	6.52	2.70
23.46	24.66	2.70	21.41	22.51	2.70	6.52	6.93	2.70
24.66	25.38	2.70	22.51	23.07	2.70	6.93	7.18	2.70
25.38	28.01	2.70	23.07	23.84	2.70	7.18	7.72	2.70
28.01	29.79	2.70	23.84	28.58	2.70	7.72	7.81	2.70
29.79	34.46	2.70	28.58	28.7	2.70	7.81	8	2.70
Range		Probability	Range		Probability	Range		Probability
34.46	39.67	2.70	28.7	30.55	2.70	8	8.37	2.70
39.67	39.88	2.70	30.55	31.49	2.70	8.37	8.8	2.70
39.88	43.46	2.70	31.49	32.16	2.70	8.8	9.85	2.70
43.46	44.63	2.70	32.16	32.42	2.70	9.85	10.38	2.70
44.63	52.82	2.70	32.42	33.36	2.70	10.38	10.54	2.70
52.82	57.36	2.70	33.36	37.2	2.70	10.54	11.24	2.70
57.36	60.7	2.70	37.2	37.43	2.70	11.24	14.71	2.70

Source: GAO calculation.

Table 9. Cross-Correlation and Serial Correlation of Historical Annual Returns

	Small company	Large company	U.S. Treasury bills
Small company	1		
Large company	0.66	1	
U.S. Treasury bills	-0.01	0.05	1
Serial correlation	-0.003	0.03	· 0.81

Source: GAO calculation.

Table 10. Annual Compounded Returns and Standard Deviations for Large Company and Small Company Stocks and for U.S. Treasury Bills (in percentage), 1970–2007

	Small company	Large company	U.S. Treasury bills
Compounded nominal returns	13	11	6
Standard deviation	23	17	3
Strategic asset allocation in Palau trust fund[a]	15	50	35

Source: GAO analysis based on Ibbotson 2008 Yearbook.

[a] This was the strategic asset allocation as of September 2007. It may change over time.

Cross-correlation and serial correlation are built into the Monte Carlo random draws to capture the co-movement across the asset classes and over time. (See table 9.)

The annual compounded returns and standard deviations for the various asset classes are shown in the table 10.

Monte Carlo Simulation Results

Each year's return is randomly selected from the return distribution of each asset class. The simulation is run 10,000 times, yielding 10,000 possible outcomes and providing a distribution of annual investment income, account balance, and disbursements. (Table 11 shows the first 20 trial values from the simulation of the trust fund account balance.)

Table 11. Trial Values of the Palau Trust Fund Balance, 2025–2044

(Dollars in millions)

Trial value	2025	2026	2027	2028	2029	2030	2031	2032	2033	2034
1	62	56	48	42	29	18	4	0	0	0
2	258	305	337	338	402	442	484	516	589	641
3	93	75	59	49	44	24	11	1	0	0
4	467	509	571	602	677	770	860	843	924	1,121
5	193	173	149	143	146	140	147	149	145	163
6	175	174	159	148	122	120	98	68	54	39
7	142	131	141	147	131	146	169	160	133	130
8	135	124	130	143	134	152	166	180	177	181
9	428	385	384	431	458	469	413	513	502	579
10	764	872	878	918	1,028	1,087	1,306	1,303	1,344	1,573
11	129	111	105	109	86	73	68	63	56	54
12	0	0	0	0	0	0	0	0	0	0
13	139	135	154	131	107	92	91	74	49	40
14	424	472	576	605	666	761	767	775	818	972
15	58	50	39	32	20	6	0	0	0	0
16	0	0	0	0	0	0	0	0	0	0
17	37	19	7	0	0	0	0	0	0	0
18	80	70	66	60	48	40	23	9	0	0
19	14	2	0	0	0	0	0	0	0	0
20	217	188	156	150	153	127	123	112	100	79
Median	147	144	142	140	135	130	127	122	118	112
10th per-centile	0	0	0	0	0	0	0	0	0	0
90th per-centile	416	443	469	502	536	576	612	661	708	762

Table 11. (Continued)

(Dollars in millions) Trial value	2035	2036	2037	2038	2039	2040	2041	2042	2043	2044
1	0	0	0	0	0	0	0	0	0	0
2	762	915	1,013	1,112	1,304	1,494	1,843	2,134	2,477	2,818
3	0	0	0	0	0	0	0	0	0	0
4	1,010	1,114	1,202	1,179	1,34	1,184	1,267	1,284	1,540	1,615
5	164	158	150	152	138	130	147	147	152	155
6	30	20	8	0	0	0	0	0	0	0
7	125	129	107	97	99	101	110	115	115	118
8	155	161	138	118	123	138	116	119	110	116
9	631	692	683	608	640	686	762	706	753	933
10	1,749	1,860	2,244	2,674	2,925	3,065	3,536	4,022	4,934	4,777
11	44	32	22	8	0	0	0	0	0	0
12	0	0	0	0	0	0	0	0	0	0
13	25	13	1	0	0	0	0	0	0	0
14	1,139	986	982	899	1,102	1,235	1,447	1,599	1,896	2,069
15	0	0	0	0	0	0	0	0	0	0
16	0	0	0	0	0	0	0	0	0	0
17	0	0	0	0	0	0	0	0	0	0
18	0	0	0	0	0	0	0	0	0	0
19	0	0	0	0	0	0	0	0	0	0
20	57	50	39	21	6	0	0	0	0	0
Median	106	100	93	84	75	66	56	46	34	22
10th per-centile	0	0	0	0	0	0	0	0	0	0
90th per-centile	819	887	961	1,025	1,109	1,201	1,304	1,419	1,538	1,649

Source: GAO analysis.

Note: Years cited are fiscal years (Oct. 1-Sept. 30).

Table 12. Historical Rates of Return of a Portfolio Based on the Palau Trust Fund Asset Allocation (in percentage).

Period	Nominal Returns	Rate of Inflation	Real Returns
1926-2007	8.08	3.05	4.86
1970-2007	9.08	4.62	4.29
1988-2007	8.88	3.04	5.80
1998-2007	5.23	2.68	2.52

Source: GAO calculation.

Note: To calculate the compounded returns, we used the annual nominal returns published in the Ibbotson Associates 2008 Yearbook. We rebalance the portfolio annually to maintain the asset allocation of 50 percent in U.S. large capital funds, 15 percent in U.S. small capital funds, and 35 percent in fixed income assets. The returns are net of fees and commissions, which we assume to be 1 percent annually.

Historical Returns of a Portfolio Based on Palau Trust Fund Asset Allocation with Various Time Periods

Forecasts of future returns are subject to considerable uncertainty. The historical rates of return for the asset classes held in the fund's portfolio differ depending on the time period considered, as illustrated in table 12.

APPENDIX V. COMPACT ROAD

Stakeholders responsible for building a road system on Palau encountered challenges in planning and constructing the road, including changes in the project's scope, decisions about locating the route, and difficult geographical and environmental conditions. In large part because of these challenges, the construction of a 53-mile road for Palau, which was built to U.S. standards (see figure 8), was completed 7 years later than planned. The government of Palau is now responsible for the road and faces challenges in managing and funding its operation and maintenance. Palau has made some initial efforts to maintain the road, but both U.S. and Palau officials are concerned that the government of Palau has not sufficiently funded the necessary maintenance. Without such maintenance, the road will deteriorate over time and may not provide the economic development benefits envisioned for the people of Palau.

Background

To assist Palau in its efforts to advance its economic development and self-sufficiency, the Compact of Free Association between the United States and Palau called for the United States to build a road system (compact road) in Palau according to mutually agreed-upon specifications before October 1, 2000. The road was completed and turned over to Palau on October 1, 2007.

Source: USACE.

Figure 8. Compact Road at Beginning and End of Construction.

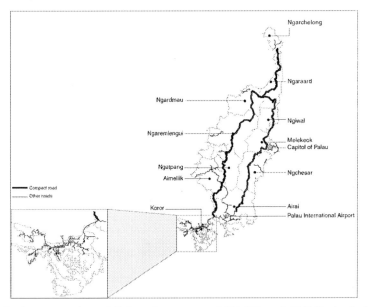

Source: GAO presentation of Palau Government, USACE, and U.S.Geological Survey data.

Figure 9. Map of Palau Roads and States.

While Interior's Office of Insular Affairs budgeted $149 million for the project, the cost incurred thus far is approximately $144 million.[80] Palau contributed to the project by preparing, negotiating, and acquiring more than 2,000 easements for the road at no cost. U.S. and Palau officials expressed their satisfaction with the completed road.[81]

Source: USACE

Figure 10. Compact Road Construction Terrain and Cut Slope Failure.

After completing the compact road, the United States turned it over to Palau, which is responsible for operating and maintaining it.[82] In August 2005, the USACE delivered a plan to Palau authorities for operating and maintaining the road. The plan provides options for Palau to develop maintenance methodologies that can result in the lowest long-term maintenance costs. The plan also provides options for developing a funding mechanism to support the operation and maintenance of the road, including a "user pays" concept.

Scope Changes, Route Location Decisions, and Difficult Geographical and Environmental Conditions Presented Challenges in Designing and Constructing the Road

According to USACE officials,[83] negotiations over the project's scope presented challenges in designing the compact road, extending the time required to finalize the design. Early in the project, Palau requested and negotiated with the United States a change that expanded the scope of the project from a 53-mile, 18-foot-wide double bituminous surface treatment road[84] with 2-foot-wide shoulders, as originally agreed, to a 53-mile, 24-foot-wide paved road with 4-foot-wide shoulders.[85] U.S. legislation passed in April 1996 authorized the Secretary of the Interior to agree to technical changes to the road, as long as the United States did not incur any additional costs, enabling U.S. and Palau stakeholders to negotiate changes to the project.[86]

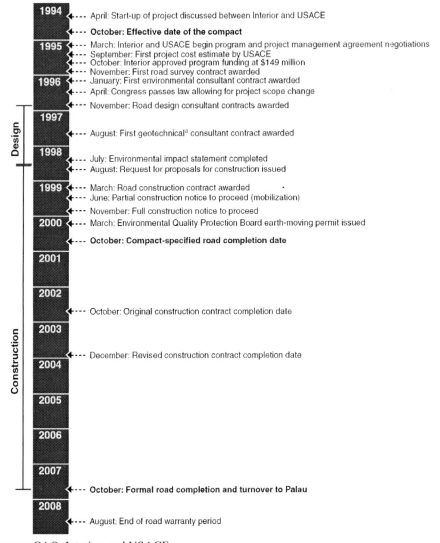

Source: GAO, Interior, and USACE.

[a] Geotechnical consultants use borings to analyze the below-ground conditions of the soil, rock, and water tables to assist road designers in determining how the road should be designed and constructed.

Figure 11. Compact Road Project Timeline.

Identifying and agreeing on an acceptable route for the compact road posed further challenges in designing the project, according to Interior and USACE officials. The route had to be approved by the government of Palau and meet engineering feasibility requirements. The government of Palau eventually decided to build a road to form a ring around the island of Babeldaob, providing road access to all 10 states on the island (see figure 9).[87] The design also includes a spur at the north end of the island.

During the project's construction, stakeholders encountered challenges associated with Palau's geographic location and environment. Getting equipment, materials, and manpower to the island on time proved difficult.[88] In addition, USACE had to arrange for the removal and destruction of 5,500 rounds of ordinance dating from World War II during construction. Palau's rugged peak and valley terrain, dense jungle, tropical weather, and poor soil quality further complicated construction efforts. For example, the valleys had to be filled and the hillsides cut in peak areas along the route to create a grade for the road consistent with U.S. standards (see figure 10). Tropical rains, combined with the high moisture content of the soils used for fill material, made it difficult to get the compaction needed to keep the pavement from settling later. In addition, the rain and poor soils together caused many landslides, referred to as cut slope failures, along the road during construction.[89] Such failures continued to occur after sections of the road were initially completed; however, according to a USACE official, there have been no new failures since October 2007, when Palau accepted the compact road and assumed responsibility for maintaining it.

Compact Road Was Completed Late but Did Not Exceed USACE's Original Cost Estimate

The compact road—which was to be completed within 6 years of October 1994, the effective date of the compact between the United States and Palau—was turned over to Palau October 2007, 13 years after the compact's effective date (see figure 11). It took almost 2 years from the effective date to award design contracts, approximately 2 years to design the project, and approximately 9 years to construct the road. When we reviewed the site, we found the road completed and open to traffic, with only a few deficiencies: For example, the road had settled at the end of one bridge and water was seeping out between the road and the adjoining shoulder at other locations. USACE is investigating the cause of the settlement to determine if it is covered by the contractor warranty. In addition, drains are being added along the road under the shoulder in water seepage areas to carry water away from the road and eliminate the seepage, which could cause future maintenance problems by weakening ground support for the road pavement.

USACE officials reported that U.S. costs for the project were within USACE's September 1995 estimate of $149 million.[90] That estimate was used to create a program budget of $25 million for design and design supervision and $124 million for construction and construction supervision. While the scope of the project was substantially increased, its costs did not exceed USACE's estimate because of what an Interior official described as a very competitive bidding environment, which allowed the construction contract to be awarded at a lower-than-expected cost. Contractors' original construction proposals ranged from $73 million to $220 million and a contract was awarded for $88.6 million. According to USACE officials, construction contract modifications have since increased the cost of the construction contract to $107.6 million. In total, USACE has expended approximately $138.8 million for the project's design and construction, and about $5.1 million in contractual obligations for design and construction work remain.[91] However, the project is currently the subject of a construction contract dispute between the United States and the construction contractor, and the final U.S. cost of the project cannot be determined until appeals by the construction contractor are resolved.[92]

Management and Funding Challenges Hinder Palau's Ongoing Efforts to Maintain the Road

Now that the government of Palau, through its Bureau of Public Works, is responsible for the compact road's operation and maintenance, it faces management and funding challenges. Palau has made initial efforts to maintain the road, but U.S. and Palau officials are concerned about Palau's ability to provide sufficient funding to maintain the road in a condition that supports the desired economic development.

U.S. Government Provided Road Maintenance Training and Operations and Maintenance Plan

Long before turning the compact road over to Palau in October 2007, the U.S. government provided Palau with training and a plan for operations and maintenance. Specifically, Interior partnered with Palau Community College in late 1999 and early 2000 to provide training in road maintenance techniques. An Interior official told us that subsequent to the initial training, Interior offered additional maintenance training using technical assistance funding, but Palau has not taken Interior up on the offer. Additionally, in August 2005, USACE—as required by the subsidiary construction projects agreement—provided Palau with the *Operation and Maintenance Plan for the Palau Compact Road*. This plan, which a USACE consultant developed primarily from information provided by an industry group that supports U.S. state highway maintenance efforts, includes a strategy and guidance for Palau to develop its own detailed program for successfully operating and maintaining the road. The plan cautions that unless Palau adopts an aggressive maintenance program, the economic development opportunities made possible by the compact road will be short lived. Moreover, according to the plan, failure to provide timely maintenance will accelerate the road's deterioration, and more expensive road reconstruction may then be required. The plan estimates annual maintenance costs for the compact road that range from $1.5 million to $3 million. Those estimates cover the costs of recurrent maintenance tasks such as mowing, sign repair, and guardrail repair; overhead such as supervisory personnel, fuel, and supplies; capital investments such as equipment and storage yards; project maintenance such as asphalt seal coat treatments; and funds for natural and man-made disasters and emergencies.[93] To minimize those costs, the plan recommends using cost-benefit analysis to develop least-cost methods of providing the operations and maintenance services. The plan also provides options for developing a funding mechanism for the operation and maintenance of the compact road including a "user pays" concept that would require the government of Palau to enact new taxes or increase existing taxes to adequately fund the road's operations and maintenance.

Palau Faces Challenges in Managing the Compact Road's Maintenance According to the Plan

The Palau Bureau of Public Works has performed some maintenance activities, but not to the degree envisioned in the plan. Specifically, Palau workers, 21 of whom are currently assigned to maintain the compact road, according to Palau officials, have used string trimmers to cut the grass and weeds alongside the road (see figure 12). During the 3-month period from November 2007 through January 2008, they trimmed approximately 15 of the compact road's 53 miles. This level of production would not allow Palau to complete the mowing along the entire compact road every 3 months as the plan recommends.

Source: GAO.

Figure 12. Grass-Cutting Crews and Damaged Guardrail.

Palau has not yet begun the full range of operation and maintenance activities set out in the plan, such as developing sign inventories, inspecting bridges, sealing cracks,[94] or requiring permits for the public to install driveways, private signs, and other obstructions in the road right-of-way. Moreover, the Bureau of Public Works could provide only limited documentation of its maintenance activities to date, and this documentation did not include records of such actions as road maintenance work orders completed, miles of grass cut, or numbers of cut slope failures cleaned up.

Our site review of the compact road found the road in very good condition except that weeds and grass were overgrowing portions of the roadway, potentially obstructing drivers' views in some places. In addition, several new private drives were being connected to the compact road that did not meet the compact road standards for private drives. In one case, a guardrail installed for safety had been removed.

Funding Challenges Limit Palau's Ability to Maintain the Road

With the compact road, the maintenance workload of the Palau Bureau of Public Works has increased, but the budget for the Bureau has decreased. The compact road has more than tripled Palau's national road miles, increasing their number from 20 to 73. Yet the budget for the Bureau of Public Works has decreased from approximately $1.7 million for 2007 to about $1.5 million for 2008.[95] For 2007, the Bureau's Bridge and Road Maintenance Branch had a budget of approximately $175,000, and that sum had not changed significantly for the last 5 years, according to a Palau official. The Ministry of Resources and Development received an additional $300,000 in its 2008 budget specifically for road maintenance. This funding is separate from funding for the Ministry's Bureau of Public Works. Palau officials indicated that they plan to use this

$300,000 for fuel, supplies, and some equipment. The plan suggests a minimum of $1.5 million annually for the maintenance of the compact road.

Besides funding routine maintenance, Palau needs to maintain sufficient resources to provide emergency maintenance in the event of a typhoon or severe rain. Such emergencies may require repairs to bridges and drainage pipes, as well as cleanups of cut slope failures, fallen trees, and other debris to make the road operational. Between January 30, 2007 and September 5, 2007, before USACE turned the compact road over to Palau, it awarded contracts totaling approximately $334,000 to clean up and repair cut slope failures along completed sections of the compact road. Such cleanups are now part of Palau's maintenance responsibility and must be done if the road is to remain safe and open to traffic. A USACE official reported that since September 5, 2007, only small soil slides have occurred at sites of previous cut slope failures, and the Bureau of Public Works cleaned these up with help from a local contractor.

Palau has considered outsourcing some critical road maintenance tasks. In May 2007, Palau authorities issued a request for proposals for activities such as mowing services for the entire compact road, cleaning of bridges and drainage structures, and inspecting culverts and bridges. Under this proposal, the contractor would provide all equipment and manpower, reducing the need for Palau to purchase equipment and hire full-time employees. We found that at least one proposal was submitted to Palau to perform these services for 1 year at a cost of $371,069. The proposal also indicated how equipment would be used and how often maintenance activities would be performed. For example, grass would be cut along the entire compact road monthly. Palau officials, however, decided not to award a contract for maintenance services. Instead, they believed they had enough public sector workers to provide maintenance services for the first year.

To help address its maintenance funding challenge, Palau has requested additional funding from the United States. In December 2007, Palau asked Interior for approximately $1 million to purchase equipment listed in the plan to mow, clean, and clear the road. When we asked a Palau official about Palau's plan for using the equipment, he said Palau does not have a specific plan for the equipment. Palau also had not considered the costs to maintain the equipment or how it would be utilized to justify its purchase and evaluate the effectiveness of its use.[96] Palau also asked the United States to set aside a $3 million debt Palau owes to the United States under section 211(b) of the compact to create a capital fund to finance the maintenance of the compact road. The U.S. Congress recently passed legislation that permits Palau to do so.[97]

Assistance in managing and funding the operation and maintenance of the compact road is available to Palau through guidance developed for local public works agencies in the United States. In contrast to the guidance for state highway agencies, on which the USACE consultant based the plan, this guidance exists for local public works agencies. With only 73 miles of road to maintain, such guidance may be more appropriate for Palau than the state guidance, and using such guidance may help Palau fine tune its compact road operations and maintenance activities and budgets. For example, the National Association of County Engineers developed a guide for maintenance management and one for road surface management. In addition, the Transportation Information Center at the University of Wisconsin, Madison, has manuals for simplified road pavement surface evaluation. The Federal Highway Administration's Local and Tribal Technical Assistance Programs also provide a clearinghouse of information and training resources for local agencies responsible for roads and bridges. Much of this information is available at no cost through the Internet.

APPENDIX VI. SELECTED FEDERAL PROGRAMS

This appendix provides additional information on discretionary federal programs with expenditures in Palau during 2006. We include additional information on selected federal programs to illustrate the diversity of U.S. federal program assistance in the areas of education, health, and infrastructure. Following the description of selected programs, Table 13 lists discretionary U.S. federal program funds expended by the Palau national government, Palau Community College, and Palau Community Action Agency, as reported in the organizations' single audit reports for 2006.

Department of Transportation: FAA Airport Improvement Program

Expenditures:

- 2005: $1.62 million
- 2006: $9.40 million

Recipient: Government of Palau

Purpose and legislation: The Vision 100-Century of Aviation Reauthorization Act (Pub. L. No. 108-176, § 188, 117 Stat. 2490, 2519 (2003)) made sponsors of airports in Palau eligible for grants from the Airport Improvement Program discretionary fund and the Small Airport Fund for 2004 through 2007. According to an Airport Improvement Program coordinator, the purpose of the Airport

Improvement Program is to create or preserve airport assets and infrastructure. The Airport Improvement Program's reauthorization for 2008-2011 is currently pending before Congress.[98] It contains language that would continue Palau's eligibility for funding through this program, and preparations are being made in Palau and at FAA to make further improvements to the airport if the bill is passed.

Program observations: According to Airport Improvement Program managers, Palau's airport runway, prior to the FAA-funded improvements, was near closure due to critical aviation safety concerns. Airport Improvement Program funds have been used to rehabilitate the runway, taxiway, and signage; rehabilitate the airport apron and install two additional loading bridges; procure two aircraft rescue and fire-fighting vehicles and one rapid intervention vehicle; construct a new aircraft rescue and fire-fighting building; install perimeter security fencing; and develop an airport master plan. Agency officials told us that the Airport Improvement Program's 4-year investment in Palau, from 2004-2007, totaled approximately $26 million. In commenting on this report, FAA noted that the FAA-funded improvements included grant assurances agreed to by the Palau government, which require continued maintenance and operations for the projected useful life of the facilities and equipment. Moreover, they said that the Palau government needs to staff the airport with trained and qualified aircraft rescue and firefighting personnel. They emphasized the need for safety at Palau's airport as U.S. carriers fly to Palau from several locations and use it as an emergency airport for overlying routes.

Both agency officials and representatives from the government of Palau cited the improvements to the safety and capacity of the airport. According to agency officials, Palau has performed well in its management of Airport Improvement Program grants because it has effectively received competitive bids for projects, made reasonable decisions, and tracked grant funds well.

Department of Education: Pell Grants

Expenditures:

- 2005: $1.83 million
- 2006: $2.19 million

Recipient: Palau Community College through individual students
Purpose and legislation: Pell Grants, from the Department of Education, are intended to provide eligible, undergraduate students with financial assistance for educational expenses. The Higher Education Act of 1965, as amended (Pub. L.

No. 89-329, 79 Stat. 1219), authorized Palau's participation.[99] Palau's continued eligibility for Pell grants after 2009 is contingent on the continued authorization of Palau's eligibility for the program in the reauthorization of the Higher Education Act.

Program observations: The Pell Grant program provides grants to eligible Palauan students, and, because of the low-income levels in Palau relative to the United States, most students qualify for the program. According to a representative from the community college, the Pell Grant program provides a valuable source of student aid and assists approximately 550 of the 600 students attending the community college. This amounts to a cost of approximately $3,987 per student receiving Pell Grant assistance.

Department of Health and Human Services: Head Start

Expenditures:

- 2005: $1.95 million
- 2006: $1.88 million

Recipient: Palau Community Action Agency

Purpose and legislation: The Head Start program is designed to provide comprehensive child development services to economically disadvantaged children and families. The program promotes school readiness by assisting low-income children, ages 3-5, with education, health, nutrition, medical, and dental services. Omnibus Budget Reconciliation Act of 1981, Pub. L. No. 97-35, § 636, 95 Stat. 499.

Program observations: Children are eligible to participate in the Head Start program based on several criteria, including income levels. According to Palau's Head Start representatives, approximately 95 percent of Palau households qualify by falling under the income level threshold, which uses U.S.-based federal income guidelines. The Head Start program plays a unique role in Palau's education system as the primary pre-school and kindergarten option for most of the nation's children. According to government of Palau statistics, approximately 82 percent of Palau's children enrolled in a pre-school or kindergarten are Head Start participants. Palau Head Start maintains 13 educational centers located in different areas throughout the country and has a funded enrollment level of 509 students, or approximately $3,697 per attending child. HHS provides approximately 80 percent of the funding for the program and the remaining 20 percent is provided through matching funds by the government of Palau or contributed as in-kind donations, such as free use of public facilities and parent volunteer hours.

Department of Education: Special Education Grants to States

Expenditures:

- 2005: $0.95 million
- 2006: $1.08 million

Recipient: Government of Palau, Ministry of Education

Purpose and legislation: The Special Education Grants to States is provided to local education agencies to help provide special education and related services needed to make a free, appropriate public education available to children with disabilities. The Individuals with Disabilities Education Act (IDEA), Pub. L. No. 91-230, § 611, as added by Pub. L. No. 108-446, § 101, 118 Stat. 2662 (2004) codified at 20 U.S.C. § 1411.

Program observations: The special education program in Palau is managed through Palau's Ministry of Education. According to Ministry of Education officials, the U.S. Department of Education is the sole source of funding for the special education program. The special education program is entirely funded through two grants: The Special Education Grant to States (Part B) and the Special Education Program for Pacific Island Entities (SEPPIE). The Special Education Grant to States program provides funding for daily operating expenses while SEPPIE funds are used for renovating special education classrooms and educating special education teachers. According to Department of Education officials, SEPPIE funds are being phased out and future funds will be provided under the Part B grant program.

Palau's Ministry of Education has used the funding to establish a special education program that serves 193 children, at a cost of approximately $5,618 per student, either part time or full time, in Palau's 16 elementary schools and one high school. In addition, the Ministry of Education has established a memorandum of understanding with the local Head Start program in order to identify and serve students with disabilities who have not yet entered the formal school system.

Department of Health and Human Services: Consolidated Health Centers

Expenditures:

- 2005: $0.56 million
- 2006: $0.62 million

Recipient: Government of Palau, Ministry of Health

Purpose and legislation: The Consolidated Health Center Program promotes the development and operation of community-based primary health care service systems in medically underserved areas and improves the health status of medically underserved populations. This is a competitive, grant-based program. Public Health Service Act, Section 330(e),(g),(h),(i), as added by Health Centers Consolidation Act of 1996, Pub. L. No. 104-299, § 2, 110 Stat. 3626, 3626-42.

Program observations: The Consolidated Health Center Program plays a supporting role in Palau's public health system. The grant originally supported 10 small dispensaries located throughout Palau, although several of the dispensaries have been consolidated to create four "Super Dispensaries" while still maintaining some of the small dispensaries on the outlying islands. During calendar year 2006, over 18,600 patients received services through the grant-supported health clinics.

Both U.S. agency officials and officials from the government of Palau report that the Consolidated Health Centers Program is important for Palau. However, a U.S. agency official stated that the program had two weaknesses in its implementation. First, the distinction between the health center and the national hospital was not clear. The officials found it difficult to tell which patients were being treated by which organization. Second, the officials said some of the dispensaries outside of Koror were inadequate to meet patients' needs in these areas.

Department of Education: Freely Associated States Education Grants

Expenditures:

- 2005: $0.57 million
- 2006: $0.55 million

Recipient: Government of Palau, Ministry of Education

Purpose and legislation: The Freely Associated States Education Grant (FASEG)[100] Program is a competitive direct grant program, provided by the Department of Education, to local education agencies in Palau and other outlying areas (American Samoa, Guam, the Commonwealth of the Northern Marianas Islands) as authorized under the Elementary and Secondary Education Act of 1965, Pub. L. No. 89-10, § 1121(b) and (c), as added by No Child Left Behind

Act of 2001, Pub. L. No. 107-110, § 101, 115 Stat. 1425, 1513 (2002) codified at 20 U.S.C. § 6331. The grant can be used for teacher training, curriculum development, instructional materials, general school improvement or reform, and direct educational services. In commenting on this report, Department of Education officials noted that Palau's continued eligibility for FASEG funds will depend on the outcome of the compact review in 2009. Under the definition of an outlying area in the No Child Left Behind Act, Palau continues to be eligible for the FASEG program until an agreement for the extension of the United States education assistance under the Compact of Free Association for each of the freely associated states becomes effective after the date of the enactment of the No Child Left Behind Act of 2001. (20 U.S.C. § 7801 (30)).

Program observations: The FASEG program assists Palau in addressing a challenge that was identified by both the U.S. agency officials and officials from Palau's Ministry of Education: improving teacher quality. According to officials in Palau's ministry, teacher qualifications have been decreasing in recent years because of mandatory retirement laws that have caused a number of older, qualified teachers to retire. FASEG funds address this issue by allowing teachers, administrators, and staff to receive training in content selection, standards and benchmarks development, teaching strategies, educational technology, and other reading and teacher quality programs. In 2006, for example, FASEG program funds were used to sponsor a range of educational events and trainings, including a Social Studies Test Items Development Workshop and a Writing and Reading Workshop.

U.S. Department of Agriculture: Rural Utilities Services Telecommunications Loan Program

Loan Amount: $39.14 million, 4.59 percent interest rate
Loan Approved: 1992
Loan Due: 2029
Recipient: Palau National Communications Corporation (PNCC)
Purpose and legislation: The Rural Electrification Act of 1936, May 20, 1936, c. 432, 49 Stat. 1363, as amended, authorized the Secretary of USDA to make loans for furnishing and improving telephone service in rural areas. The loans were intended to be used to furnish, improve, expand, construct, and operate telephone service in rural areas. USDA Rural Utilities Service made the loan to PNCC.

Program observations: PNCC, a semi-autonomous, governmental agency, took out a loan for approximately $39 million in 1992 in an effort to improve its telecommunications infrastructure. The loan is set at a 4.59 percent interest rate and will be paid in full on November 30, 2029. According to PNCC representatives, the funds were used to lay fiber-optic cable throughout Palau and construct an outside switch board and switch center. According to U.S. agency officials, the loan was secured through a government guarantee and through an established escrow fund for 1 year's debt payments. U.S. officials stated that PNCC is current on its debt and the outstanding loan balance is approximately $31 million.

Both U.S. agency officials and PNCC representatives expressed concern regarding PNCC's ability to repay its loan due to increased competition in Palau. These officials stated that PNCC is required by law to provide universal fixed-line service throughout Palau, and has used the revenue generated through its cellular, Internet, and other services to support the costs of providing universal fixed-line coverage. According to PNCC representatives, outside companies, which are not required to offer universal fixed-line service, have entered Palau's cellular and long-distance markets, which has reduced PNCC's ability to generate revenue. U.S. agency officials and PNCC representatives stated that PNCC's ability to repay its loan would be in jeopardy if it continues to lose valuable cellular and long-distance customers while maintaining expensive universal fixed-line coverage.

Department of Defense Civic Action Teams

Expenditures:

- 2005: $2.5 million
- 2006: $2.3 million

Purpose and legislation: The compact's implementing legislation, Compact of Free Association with Palau, Pub. L. No. 99-658, 100 Stat. 3672 (1986), states that "in recognition of the special development needs of Palau," the United States "shall make available" military Civic Action Teams for use in Palau under terms and conditions mutually agreed upon by the United States and Palau. An end date for the CATs is not stated.

Program observations: The CAT program provides assistance to Palau through teams of U.S. military service men and women that carry out small-scale infrastructure projects and other projects that support socioeconomic development and capacity building. CATs have been active in Palau for nearly 40 years. Teams of 13 service men and women, primarily engineers, are stationed in Palau for 6-

month rotations. The teams provide assistance in four main areas: (1) community construction, (2) apprentice training, (3) community relations, and (4) a medical program. Under the community construction program, the CAT members complete small-scale infrastructure projects such as renovating community centers, maintaining roads, and building basketball courts. Members of the local population—frequently Palau's state governments—request specific projects and pay for the raw materials. DOD officials stated that occasionally DOD purchased the raw materials because of the difficulty in securing funding from the project's sponsor in Palau. In 2007, CATs in Palau did community construction projects across Palau; the projects had a presence in each of Palau's 16 states. While conducting these projects, the CATs work with local trainees in an apprentice program. These trainees learn construction and mechanic trades; others learn administrative or medical skills. CAT members assist apprentices with job placement at the end of the program. CAT members host community events such as movie nights and tutoring in the local schools. Finally, the CAT team offers a free medical clinic to the entire community, plus medical outreach to outlying states. DOD officials in both Palau and Guam, where operational support is conducted, reported that the CATs give U.S. military men and women the opportunity to do humanitarian work in a welcoming, positive environment. They said the teams are highly visible in Palau and are viewed positively by the local population.

Table 13. Discretionary Federal Program Funds Expended in Palau, 2006

U.S. Agency	Federal Program	2006 Expenditure	Palau Recipient
DOT-FAA	Airport Improvement Program	$ 9,400,475	Palau National Government
DOT-FAA	**Total 2006 Program Expenditures**	**$ 9,400,475**	
HHS	Head Start	$ 1,881,677	Palau Community Action Agency
HHS	Centers for Disease Control and Prevention—Investigations and Technical Assistance	$ 1,484,325	Palau National Government
HHS	Consolidated Health Centers	$ 618,157	Palau National Government
HHS	Substance Abuse and Mental Health Services—Projects of Regional and National Significance	$ 309,518	Palau National Government
HHS	National Bioterrorism Hospital Preparedness Program	$ 301,596	Palau National Government
HHS	Maternal and Child Health Federal Consolidated Programs	$ 269,298	Palau National Government

Table 13. (Continued)

U.S. Agency	Federal Program	2006 Expenditure	Palau Recipient
HHS	Epidemiologic Research Studies of Acquired Immunodeficiency Syndrome (AIDS) and Human Immunodeficiency Virus (HIV) Infection in Selected Population Groups	$ 207,265	Palau National Government
HHS	Basic/Core Area Health and Education Center	$ 198,255	Palau Community College
HHS	Maternal and Child Health Services Block Grant to the States	$197,092	Palau National Government
HHS	Family Planning Services	$140,969	Palau National Government
HHS	Block Grants for Prevention and Treatment of Substance Abuse	$106,452	Palau National Government
HHS	Cooperative Agreements to Support Comprehensive School Health Programs to Prevent the Spread of HIV and Other Important Health Problems	$101,734	Palau National Government
HHS	Project Grants and Cooperative Agreements for Tuberculosis Control Program	$99,112	Palau National Government
HHS	Universal Newborn Hearing Screening	$80,257	Palau National Government
HHS	Immunization Grants	$77,287	Palau National Government
HHS	Consolidated Knowledge Development and Application Program	$76,466	Palau National Government
HHS	Cooperative Agreements for State-based Diabetes Control Programs and Evaluation and Surveillance Systems	$67,858	Palau National Government
HHS	HIV Care Formula Grants	$64,628	Palau National Government
HHS	Block Grants for Community Mental Health Services	$50,355	Palau National Government
HHS	Preventive Health Services—Sexually Transmitted Disease Control Grants	$30,737	Palau National Government
HHS	Preventive Health and Health Services Block Grant	$22,684	Palau National Government
HHS	Human Immunodeficiency Virus (HIV)/ Acquired Immunodeficiency Virus Syndrome (AIDS) Surveillance	$17,790	Palau National Government
HHS	Civil Rights and Privacy Rule Compliance Activities	$11,004	Palau National Government
HHS	Injury Prevention and Control Research and State and Community Based Programs	$2,500	Palau National Government
HHS	**Total 2006 Program Expenditures**	**$6,417,016**	
Education	Pell Grant	$2,193,038	Palau Community College

U.S. Agency	Federal Program	2006 Expenditure	Palau Recipient
Education	Special Education Grants to States	$899,881	Palau National Government
Education	Freely Associated States Education Grant Program	$549,401	Palau National Government
Education	Upward Bound Program	$359,618	Palau Community College
Education	Upward Bound Math and Science Program	$207,487	Palau Community College
Education	Talent Search	$203,054	Palau Community College
Education	Special Education Grants to States	$184,386	Palau National Government
Education	Student Support Services Program	$182,819	Palau Community College
Education	Gaining Early Awareness and Readiness for Undergraduate Programs	$171,833	Palau National Government
Education	Vocational Education Basic Grants to States	$153,304	Palau National Government
Education	Teacher Quality Enhancement Grants	$103,527	Palau National Government
Education	Federal Work Study	$90,439	Palau Community College
Education	Minority Science	$87,899	Palau Community College
Education	Supplemental Educational Opportunity Grant	$73,231	Palau Community College
Education	Vocational Education Occupational and Employment Information State Grants	$53,241	Palau National Government
Education	Adult Education State Grant Program	$53,105	Palau National Government
Education	Byrd Honors Scholarships	$9,000	Palau National Government
Education	**Total 2006 Program Expenditures**	**$5,575,263**	
Interior	Economic, Social, and Political Development of the Territories[a]	$2,152,320	Palau National Government
Interior	**Total 2006 Program Expenditures**	**$2,152,320**	
Labor	Workforce Investment Act Dislocated Workers Program	$159,027	Palau National Government
Labor	Workforce Investment Act Youth Activities	$110,150	Palau National Government
Labor	Workforce Investment Act Adult Program	$84,400	Palau National Government

Table 13. (Continued)

U.S. Agency	Federal Program	2006 Expenditure	Palau Recipient
Labor	**Total 2006 Program Expenditures**	**$ 353,577**	
Commerce	Special Oceanic and Atmospheric Projects	$282,528	Palau National Government
Commerce	Unallied Management Projects	$42,333	Palau National Government
Commerce	National Oceanic and Atmospheric Administration Donation to IRC Meeting	$24,300	Palau National Government
Commerce	**Total 2006 Program Expenditures**	**$ 349,161**	
USDA	Cooperative Forestry Assistance	$171,757	Palau National Government
USDA	Community Facilities Loans and Grants	$70,619	Palau National Government
USDA	U.S. Department of Agriculture	$6,610	Palau Community College
USDA	**Total 2006 Program Expenditures**	**$ 248,986**	
Energy	State Energy Program	$ 423	Palau National Government
Energy	**Total 2006 Program Expenditures**	**$423**	
All Agencies	**Total 2006 Program Expenditures**	**$24,497,221**	

Source: Palau national government, Palau Community College, and Palau Community Action Agency single audit reports for 2006.

[a] Interior's programs titled "Economic, Social, and Political Development of the Territories" were summed and presented as a single program in this table. This number does not include compact direct assistance or compact road funding provided by Interior to the government of Palau.

APPENDIX VII. COMPACT ASSISTANCE PROVIDED BY THE DEPARTMENT OF THE INTERIOR

The following table was taken from the Department of the Interior's Office of Insular Affairs budget justification for 2009. It provides details on the yearly estimated payments by Interior to Palau over the first 15 years of the compact. As illustrated by the table, more than half of the compact direct assistance was provided in the first three years of the compact. The table also includes information on the compact road funding.

Table 14. Compact Assistance Provided by the Department of the Interior, Estimated Payments, 1995–2009

(Dollars in thousands)	Fiscal Year						
Activity (P.L. 99-658)	1995	1996	1997	1998	1999	2000	2001
Sect. 211(a) Current Account	12,000	12,000	12,000	12,000	7,000	7,000	7,000
Sect. 211(b) Energy Production	28,000						
Sect. 211(c) Communi-cations	1,650	150	150	150	150	150	150
Sect. 211(d) Maritime Surveillance, Health, Scholarships	631	631	631	631	631	631	631
Sect. 211(e) Start- up for 211(d)	667						
Sect. 211(f) Investment Fund[a]	66,000		4,000				
Subtotal Sec. 211	**108,948**	**12,781**	**16,781**	**12,781**	**7,781**	**7,781**	**7,781**
Activity (P.L. 99-658)	1995	1996	1997	1998	1999	2000	2001
Sect. 212(b) Capital Account	36,000						
Sect. 213 Defense Use Impact	5,500						
Sect. 215 Inflation Adjustment	35,719	5,842	6,075	6,440	3,790	3,861	4,004
Subtotal	**186,167**	**18,623**	**22,856**	**19,221**	**11,571**	**11,642**	**11,785**
Sect. 221(b) Special Block Grant	6,300	4,900	3,500	2,000	2,000	2,000	2,000
Direct payments	**192,467**	**23,523**	**26,356**	**21,221**	**13,571**	**13,642**	**13,785**
Federal services[b]	0	0	0	0	0	0	0
Sect. 212(a) Palau Road Construction	53,000		96,000				
Grand total, Palau	**245,467**	**23,523**	**122,356**	**21,221**	**13,571**	**13,642**	**13,785**

Table 14. (Continued)

(Dollars in thousands)					Fiscal Year					
Activity (P.L. 99-658)	**2002**	**2003**	**2004**	**2005**	**2006**	**2007**	**2008**	**2009**	**Totals**
Sect. 211(a) Current Account	7,000	7,000	7,000	6,000	6,000	6,000	6,000	6,000	120,000
Sect. 211(b) Energy Production									28,000
Sect. 211(c) Communi-cations	150	150	150	150	150	150	150	150	3,750
Sect. 211(d) Maritime Surveillance, Health, Scholarships	631	631	631	631	631	631	631	631	9,465
Sect. 211(e) Start- up for 211(d)									667
Sect. 211(f) Investment Fund[a]									70,000
Subtotal Sec. 211	**7,781**	**7,781**	**7,781**	**6,781**	**6,781**	**6,781**	**6,781**	**6,781**	**231,882**
Activity (P.L. 99-658)	**2002**	**2003**	**2004**	**2005**	**2006**	**2007**	**2008**	**2009**	**Totals**
Sect. 212(b) Capital Account									36,000
Sect. 213 Defense Use Impact									5,500
Sect. 215 Inflation Adjustment	4,147	4,147	4,290	3,752	3,936	4,121	4,305	4,490	98,917
Subtotal	**11,928**	**11,928**	**12,071**	**10,533**	**10,717**	**10,902**	**11,086**	**11,271**	**372,299**
Sect. 221(b) Special Block Grant	2,000	2,000	2,000	2,000	2,000	2,000	2,000	2,000	38,700
Direct payments	**13,928**	**13,928**	**14,071**	**12,533**	**12,717**	**12,902**	**13,086**	**13,271**	**410,999**
Federal services[b]	0	0	0	0	0	0	0	0	0
Sect. 212(a) Palau Road Construction									149,000
Grand total, Palau	**13,928**	**13,928**	**14,071**	**12,533**	**12,717**	**12,902**	**13,086**	**13,271**	**559,999**

Source: Department of the Interior, Office of Insular Affairs.

[a] Palau may withdraw $5 million annually from the fund in years 5 through 15.

[b] Aggregate amount included on the FSM/RMI Compact Estimated Amounts table for federal services for FSM/RMI/Palau.

APPENDIX VIII. COMMENTS FROM THE DEPARTMENT OF INTERIOR

THE ASSOCIATE DEPUTY SECRETARY OF THE INTERIOR
WASHINGTON

MAY 2 8 2008

Mr. David Gootnik
Director, International Affairs and Trade
United States Government Accountability Office
441 G Street, NW
Washington D.C. 20548

Dear Mr. Gootnik:

Thank you for the opportunity to review and comment on the draft Government Accountability Office Report entitled, "*COMPACT OF FREE ASSOCIATION: Palau's Use of and Accountability for U.S. Assistance and Prospects for Economic Self-Sufficiency*," (GAO-08-732). The Department of the Interior finds the Report very useful as we prepare for the required Compact review between the United States and Palau. The Report provides key information upon which to discuss future Executive Branch policy.

The Department accepts the recommendation to formally consult with Palau regarding Palau's financial management challenges and to assist Palau in building financial management capacity. We have already had preliminary discussions with our training partner, the U.S. Department of Agriculture Graduate School, to implement a program of leadership and succession planning for key positions in the island governments. We will address Palau's needs specifically as part of the Compact review.

Thank you again for the opportunity to comment on the Report. If you have any questions concerning the response, please communicate with Nikolao Pula, Director of the Office of Insular Affairs, at (202) 208-4736.

Sincerely,

James E. Cason

James E. Cason

APPENDIX IX. COMMENTS FROM THE REPUBLIC OF PALAU

Republic of Palau
Office of the President

Tommy E. Remengesau, Jr.
President

P.O. Box 6051, Palau, PW 96940
Tel. (680) 767-2403/2828
Fax. (680) 767-2424/1662
email IN:rop.president@palaunet.com

May 13, 2008
Serial No. 08-117

David B. Gootnick
Director, International Affairs and Trade
U.S. Government Accountability Office
441 G Street N.W.
Washington D.C. 20548

      Subject: Response to Draft GAO Report No. GAO-08-732

Dear Mr. Gootnick:

Along with appropriate Executive Branch staff, I have reviewed your draft GAO Report, dated June 2008, and, on behalf of the President of the Republic of Palau, make the comments that follow. I intend to limit my comments to issues that are appropriately related to the scope of the Daft Report, which included (1) the provision of Compact and other U.S. assistance to Palau in 1995-2009, (2) Palau's and U.S. agencies' efforts to provide accountability over Palau's use of federal funds in 1995-2006, and (3) Palau's prospects for achieving economic self-sufficiency.

I.   1995-2009 Compact Assistance

In general terms, Palau concurs with the economic analyses and figures set forth in the Draft Report. Palau would, however stress that Palau entered the Compact period in a position of extreme reliance on United States assistance. Total assistance flows in the initial years of the Compact were exceptionally high relative to the size of the economy and were in excess of 36 percent of GDP and represented roughly 64 percent of current expenditures at that time. Since that time, Palau has gradually—but persistently—become less reliant. As of Fiscal Year 2007, total United States assistance was equal to approximately 16 percent of GDP (inclusive of the $5 million drawdown allowed from the Compact Trust Fund), and United States assistance represented 41 percent of current expenditures.

II.   Accountability

In the area of accountability, Palau once again concurs with the general findings of the Draft Report. Palau has, indeed, made significant progress, as reflected in recent single audit reports. In fact, Palau was the first of the insular and FAS governments to achieve

David B. Gootnick
Subject: Response to Draft GAO Report No. GAO-08-732
5/13/2008

an unqualified audit opinion of its financial statements; having achieved that in Fiscal Year 2003 and in each subsequent year.

That being said, Palau also recognizes that there are factors related to continuing fiscal constraints that hinder our ability to sustain the progress that we have made. Despite the fact that the Office of Insular Affairs, within the Department of Interior, has provided support to Palau's on-going efforts to improve its financial management capacity through the PITI/VITI Program (Pacific Islands Training Initiative/Virgin Islands Training Initiative) and the FMIP (Financial Management Improvement Program), the inability of the Ministry of Finance to recruit and maintain qualified personnel associated with ongoing fiscal constraints, as well as the non-competitive civil service compensation, creates significant challenges for the Republic.

Palau agrees with the report finding that documentation of required annual economic consultations was lacking; however, Palau did benefit significantly from nearly annual economic consultations and did take those meetings as opportunities to address important economic performance and policy matters. Perhaps even more benefit was derived from our ongoing, but informal, interactions with lead U.S. government officials. In the future, Palau will undertake to take the lead on documenting mandated consultations for the record, so that Palau will ensure full compliance with current and future Compact requirements.

Palau also supports the Draft Report's recommendation for the Office of Insular Affairs (OIA) to continue to assist Palau in building financial management capacity. However, for this assistance to be effective, Palau intends to establish an on-going institutional strengthening program that focuses on human resource development and improved retention of key personnel to insure that financial management improvements are sustainable.

III.   Achieving Self Sufficiency

Once again, the Republic concurs with the primary findings of the Draft Report relating to Palau's prospects for achieving economic self-sufficiency. While Palau has made real progress over the last fourteen years on overall reliance on U.S. direct and federal funding assistance, these funding sources remain a significant and critical funding resource to the Republic, particularly for health and education program expenditures. Taken together, the loss of direct assistance, as partially replaced by annual Trust Fund withdrawals, the potential loss of discretionary federal programs and the potential loss of federal services (postal, weather and aviation services) would have a dramatic negative impact on Palau's efforts to continue to move towards self-sufficiency.

David B. Gootnick
Subject: Response to Draft GAO Report No. GAO-08-732
5/13/2008

In addition, Palau concurs with the Report's analysis of the Trust Fund and its potential depletion after 2016. Combined with the adverse impact from the diminishing inflation-adjusted value of the Trust Fund, failure to sufficiently capitalize the Trust Fund could lead to dire economic consequences.

Regarding the issue of fiscal reform, Palau recognizes that ultimate self-sufficiency can only result from the effective implementation of rigorous economic reforms. As part of an overall structural reform program, Palau is currently looking to establish a medium-term fiscal framework that, assuming a recapitalized Trust Fund, over ten years, calls for operational expenditure reductions and domestic revenue increases that, together, will result in current expenditures being funded primarily from domestic resources.

Finally, Palau understands that the private sector will need to grow to offset and support overall economic growth in the face of necessary fiscal adjustments over the medium-to-long term. As employment in public administration contracts and as current government expenditures decline as a share of GDP, an enhanced private sector policy framework will be needed to support private sector expansion. Policy commitments in this regard will likely include:

- Undertaking comprehensive tax reform;
- Overhauling foreign investment regulations;
- Reviewing and reforming the legal system for commercial activities;
- Reforming the financial market;
- Land reform; and
- Articulating and implementing high end tourism policies.

Palau understands that a number of issues are beyond the scope of your report. In particular, Palau would note that there are important strategic and economic benefits to the United States from (a) Palau's contributions as a strong ally of the United States in security and diplomatic matters including the U.S. military service of its youth and its strategic location in the Pacific and (b) the significant world wide leadership that Palau provides on environmental matters, particularly those related to preservation of its maritime treasures. The economic costs of these efforts are not directly reflected in Palau's economic performance or the scope of the GAO report.

David B. Gootnick
Subject: Response to Draft GAO Report No. GAO-08-732
5/13/2008

On behalf of President Tommy E. Remengesau, Jr., I would like to thank you and the staff of the GAO for its very thorough analysis of the issues relating to Palau presented in your report to the U.S. Congress. If you have any further questions regarding these very pressing issues, please feel free to present them for our immediate response.

Sincerely,

Billy G. Kuartei
Chief of Staff
Republic of Palau

APPENDIX X. STAFF ACKNOWLEDGMENTS

Staff Acknowledgment

In addition to the individual named above, Emil Friberg, Assistant Director; Kate Brentzel; Ming Chen; Cheryl Clark; Leslie Locke; Matthew Reilly; Kendall Schaefer; and Doris Yanger made key contributions to this report. Reid Lowe and Grace Lui provided technical assistance.

End Notes

[1] Unless otherwise noted, all years cited are fiscal years (Oct. 1-Sept. 30). Because the compact entered into force on Oct. 1, 1994, U.S. assistance under the compact began in fiscal year 1995.

[2] The compact's federal programs and services agreement establishes the terms under which the U.S. government provides compact federal services—postal, weather, and aviation—to Palau (see *Federal Programs and Services Agreement Concluded Pursuant to Article II of Title Two and Section 232 of the Compact of Free Association*). The agreement, which took effect in 1995, expires at the end of 2009; unless it is renewed or extended, the provision of compact federal services will not continue. The agreement sets up the legal status of programs and related services, federal agencies, U.S. contractors, and personnel of U.S. agencies implementing both

compact federal services and discretionary federal programs. The agreement does not mandate the provision of discretionary programs in Palau. U.S. legislation establishes Palau's eligibility for these programs, with funding for the programs appropriated by Congress. The impact of the agreement's expiration in 2009 on discretionary programs' operation in Palau is uncertain. The level of discretionary federal program funding after 2009 also depends on Palau's program eligibility status and the availability of appropriations; changes in either factor may increase or reduce the amounts received.

[3] *Agreement Concerning Procedures for the Implementation of United States Economic Assistance, Programs and Services Provided in the Compact of Free Association Between the Government of the United States and the Government of the Republic of Palau.*

[4] The compact required the United States to set up the trust fund with an initial investment of $66 million in 1995 and an additional $4 million in 1997. The compact stated that the trust fund's objective was to produce an average annual distribution of $15 million starting in 2010 for 35 years. It also stated that $5 million shall be distributed annually from the fund for Palau's current account operations and maintenance, starting in 1999. Under the compact's trust fund agreement, Palau, in its management of the fund, agreed to be guided by distributions set forth in a table, which set forth goals for the minimum and maximum amounts of annual distribution (see *Agreement Between the Government of the United States and the Government of Palau Regarding Economic Assistance Concluded Pursuant to Section 211(f) of the Compact of Free Association*).

[5] The National Weather Service is part of the National Oceanic and Atmospheric Administration within the Department of Commerce.

[6] In this report, "compact direct assistance" refers to the grants enumerated in sections 211-215 and section 221(b) of the compact. For further details, see table 2.

[7] All dollar amounts in this report are in current (i.e., nominal) dollars.

[8] All trust fund return rates in this report are net of fees and commissions, unless otherwise stated.

[9] In 1994, the United Nations concluded that the United States had satisfactorily discharged its obligations as administering authority of the Trust Territory of the Pacific Islands.

[10] After growing strongly in the first few years of the compact, Palau's GDP declined in 1999 and stagnated until 2003 due, in part, to negative impact on its tourism sector from the 1999 Asian Financial Crisis and the September 11, 2001 terrorism attacks. Growth resumed in 2004. Per capita GDP estimates include both Palauan-born citizens and foreign workers.

[11] This estimate excludes substantial in-kind foreign assistance from donors, often for infrastructure projects. Foreign-funded projects include the U.S.-funded compact road, the Japanese-funded Friendship Bridge connecting Babeldaob to Koror, and the Taiwanese-funded agricultural technical mission.

[12] Data on foreign workers are from Palau's Social Security office and exclude workers not registered with the office.

[13] *See Proclamation 6726 Placing into Full Force and Effect the Compact of Free Association with the Republic of Palau*, 59 Fed. Reg. 49777 (Sept. 27, 1994).

[14] The 15-year term is from 1995 to 2009.

[15] The U.S. government may audit the funds directly or use an external public auditor; in either case, the audits are conducted at no cost to the government of Palau. The U.S. government's authority to audit compact funds continues for at least 3 years after the last element of assistance has been provided and expended.

[16] All nonfederal entities that expend more than a threshold amount ($500,000 as of 2004) in federal awards in a year are required to obtain an annual audit in accordance with the Single Audit Act, codified, as amended at 31 U.S.C. Chp. 75. Single audits are audits of the recipient organization—in Palau, the national government and other component units—that focus on the recipient's financial statements, internal controls, and compliance with laws and regulations governing federal grants. One of the objectives of the act is to promote sound financial management, including effective internal controls, with respect to federal expenditures of the recipient organization. Single audit reports include the auditor's opinion on the audited financial

statements and a report on the internal controls related to financial reporting. The single audit reports also include the auditor's opinion on compliance with requirements of major federal programs and a report on internal controls related to compliance with laws, regulations, and the provisions of contracts or grant agreements.

[17] Office of Management and Budget (OMB) Circular No. A-133, *Audits of States, Local Governments, and Non-Profit Organizations*, establishes policies for federal agencies to use in implementing the Single Audit Act and provides an administrative foundation for consistent and uniform audit requirements for nonfederal entities administering federal awards.

[18] Although all federal awarding agencies are responsible for ensuring that single audit reports are completed in accordance with OMB Circular No. A-133 and are received in a timely manner, one of the award-making agencies—usually the agency that provides the largest amount of funding—is designated as the cognizant agency, with specific responsibilities under OMB Circular No. A-133. Cognizant agencies' additional responsibilities include coordinating management decisions for audit findings that affect the audit programs of more than one agency and considering auditee requests for extensions to the due dates of the reports.

[19] As a member of Palau's audit resolution team, the Office of the Public Auditor is responsible for (a) monitoring each affected agency with a single audit finding or questioned cost, (b) performing follow-up on corrective actions, and (c) reporting to Interior's OIG regarding audit findings and questioned costs that have been effectively resolved. The Office of the Public Auditor also is involved in ensuring that Palau's component units finalize their audits in time for inclusion in Palau's single audit report.

[20] Other U.S. agencies' discretionary federal grant programs have accountability requirements that are specific to those programs. We did not assess Palau's compliance with these requirements. However, Palau's expenditure of federal grants is included in the single audits; these audits review Palau's compliance with federal program requirements.

[21] According to Executive Order 12569 of 1986, *reprinted in* 51 Fed. Reg. 37171 (Oct. 16, 1986), Interior is responsible for ensuring that the economic and financial assistance provided by the compact is made available to Palau as well as for monitoring any program or activity provided to Palau by all U.S. agencies except DOD; State is responsible for government-to-government relations between the United States and Palau.

[22] Palau is required to submit these economic development plans every 5 years during the duration of title two of the compact.

[23] Title three of the compact also includes a requirement for consultations between the United States and Palau. It requires the U.S. and Palau governments to establish a joint committee to discuss any disputes over the security and defense provisions of the compact. The joint committee is required to meet semiannually unless otherwise mutually agreed.

[24] Some of the financial data presented for discretionary federal programs in this report were extracted from Palau's audited financial statements for 1995-2006; the statements for 1995-2002 received qualified opinions from external auditors. Therefore, these figures are subject to the limitations cited by the auditors in their opinions and to the material internal control weaknesses identified.

[25] The compact states that the amounts specified in sections 211-215 are "backed by the full faith and credit of the United States," which legally guarantees funding.

[26] Palau includes an account of its implementation of direct assistance in the compact annual reports it submits to the U.S. government.

[27] Although the compact states that Palau shall receive $2 million per year in 211(b) funding, a related agreement—*Agreement Concerning Special Programs Related to the Entry into Force of the Compact of Free Association Between the Government of the United States and the Government of the Republic of Palau*—specified that the United States would fulfill this commitment with a lump sum deposit of $28 million in the first year the compact went into effect, i.e. fiscal year 1995, plus an inflation adjustment of $12 million. The agreement requires Palau to pay $3 million to the United States by September 30, 2005, as a net economic cost to the United States for making the $28 million available to Palau in the first year of the compact. In its 2005 annual report, Palau reported that an official request had been made to utilize the $3 million to establish

a capital fund for compact road maintenance. The U.S. Congress recently passed legislation that permits Palau to retain the $3 million to set up a trust fund for compact road maintenance, as long as the fund is established and operated pursuant to an agreement entered into between the U.S. government and the government of Palau. See Pub. L. No. 110-229, Title VIII, Sec. 808, 122 Stat. 874 (May 8, 2008).

[28] Section 215 states that the amounts stated in sections 211(a), 211(b), 211(c), and 212(b) shall be adjusted for each fiscal year by the percent which equals two-thirds of the percentage change in the United States Gross National Product Implicit Price Deflator, or 7 percent, whichever is less in any 1 year, using fiscal year 1981 as the base.

[29] These services are provided under section 221 of title two of the compact. The United States provides in-kind contributions for the postal and aviation services and reimburses the government of Palau for the cost of operating its weather station.

[30] Palau operates its own postal service for internal mail distribution, and transports mail to and from air and sea ports for international shipment, at which point USPS takes responsibility.

[31] The federal programs and services agreement states that after the effective date of the compact, USPS may establish cost-related rates for mail from the United States to Palau. A USPS official said that State officials told USPS that raising the rates could have a negative effect on the compact's goal of establishing Palau's economic self-sufficiency, so USPS kept the postal rates the same as U.S. domestic rates.

[32] USPS relies on contracted commercial air service for airmail shipment to Palau.

[33] FAA provides the following services to Palau: en-route air traffic control from the Oakland, California airport, maintenance of nondirectional beacon and distance measuring equipment at Palau's airport; maintenance of precision approach path indicator lighting system and runway end identifier lights at Palau's airport; flight inspection of airport navigational aids; development of instrument approach and departure procedures; and technical assistance and training.

[34] This figure is based, in part, on information obtained in the single audits for 1995 through 2006 for the three primary recipients of U.S. federal grants in Palau: the Palau national government, the Palau Community College, and the Palau Community Action Agency. At the time of this report, audited financial data for 2007 were not yet available.

[35] The Palau Community College is the only postsecondary school in Palau.

[36] TRIO grant-based programs are educational and opportunity outreach programs designed to support students from disadvantaged backgrounds.

[37] The Upward Bound program, part of the TRIO programs, is designed to provide support for participants to succeed in their precollege and higher education pursuits.

[38] According to U.S. agency officials, the Palau Community Action Agency has been the sole grantee and Head Start service provider for the 40 years the program has existed in Palau.

[39] With the exception of DOD's CAT program, our analysis did not quantify the value of this additional U.S. assistance and it is not included in the discretionary federal program total of $266.7 million in figure 3 or U.S. agency expenditures in figure 4.

[40] We did not attempt to estimate the cost of Peace Corps's presence in Palau from 1995-2009.

[41] Our analysis did not attempt to quantify the value of U.S. agency-provided development loans, and this value is not included in the discretionary federal program total of $266.7 million in figure 3 or U.S. agency expenditures in figure 4.

[42] Under the Single Audit Act, the single audit reporting package is generally required to be submitted to the Federal Audit Clearinghouse, which is an automated database of single audit information, either 30 days after the receipt of the auditor's report or 9 months after the end of the period under audit.

[43] At the time of this report, Palau's fiscal year 2007 single audit report had not been submitted and is not due for submission until June 30, 2008.

[44] Auditors are required by the Single Audit Act and OMB Circular No. A-133 to provide an opinion (or disclaimers of opinion, as appropriate) as to whether financial statements are presented fairly in all material respects in conformity with generally accepted accounting principles. Generally

accepted accounting principles are the conventions, rules, and procedures that provide the norm for fair presentation of financial statements. Auditors render a qualified opinion when they identify one or more specific matters that affect the fair presentation of the financial statements. The effect of the auditors' qualified opinion can be significant enough to reduce the usefulness and reliability of the financial statements.

[45] Sound internal control over financial reporting is needed to adequately safeguard assets; ensure that transactions are properly recorded; and prevent or detect fraud, waste, and abuse.

[46] The 2006 single audit report cited five material weaknesses and nine reportable conditions in internal control over financial reporting. Reportable conditions are related to significant deficiencies in the design or operation of internal controls that could adversely affect the audited entity's ability to produce financial statements that fairly represent the entity's financial condition. Material weaknesses are reportable conditions in which the design or operation of internal controls does not reduce to a relatively low level the risk that misstatements caused by error or fraud—material in relation to the financial statements being audited—may occur and not be detected in a timely period by employees in the normal course of performing their duties. The material weaknesses cited in the 2006 report included (1) lack of supporting documentation to support travel expenditures; (2) lack of review of monthly bank reconciliations and nonresolution of reconciling differences; (3) lack of policies and procedures to reconcile accounts receivable and prepayments; and (4) lack of adherence to prescribed travel policies and procedures.

[47] In addition to requiring auditors to assess financial statements, the Single Audit Act and OMB Circular No. A-133 require auditors to determine and express an opinion as to whether the auditee has complied with laws, regulations, and the provisions of contracts or grant agreements that may have a direct and material effect on each of its major federal programs. Auditors are to identify the applicable compliance requirements to be tested and reported on in a single audit. OMB's Compliance Supplement lists and describes the types of compliance requirements and related audit objectives and suggested audit procedures that auditors should consider in single audits conducted in accordance with OMB Circular No. A-133. When auditors identify instances of noncompliance, they are required to report whether the noncompliance could have a direct and material effect on a major federal program.

[48] Of the internal control weaknesses reported in 2006, 15 were reportable conditions and 1 was considered material. In the context of compliance, reportable conditions are matters that come to an auditor's attention related to significant deficiencies in the design or operation of internal controls over compliance that could adversely affect the entity's ability to operate a major federal program within the applicable requirements of laws, regulations, contracts, and grants. Material weaknesses in this context are reportable conditions in which internal controls do not reduce to a relatively low level the risk of noncompliance with applicable requirements of laws, regulations, contracts, and grants that would be material to the major federal program being audited and undetected in a timely way by employees in the normal course of performing their duties.

[49] The 2006 report stated that this particular weakness is caused by a decentralized, fixed asset accounting division that appears to be disassociated from the rest of the accounting function, resulting in a process with little coordination, review, and monitoring.

[50] According to the 2006 single audit report, Palau's plans to address the report's findings about its compliance with, and internal control over compliance with, federal program requirements also include reconciling, reporting, and resolving differences related to its federal grants receivable balances with federal grantor agencies; ensuring that expenditures charged to federal programs are directly related to program goals and objectives; strengthening internal controls over program budget documentation, to ensure budgeted allotments agree with program objectives; and improving compliance with period of federal grant availability requirements.

[51] DOD officials also reported, and provided documentation of, annual meetings between DOD and the government of Palau to discuss security and defense issues pertinent to title three of the compact. The DOD officials said that the U.S. and Palau governments had agreed to hold the

meetings annually, instead of semiannually as required by the compact and that recent meetings were held in Palau, Guam, and Hawaii.

[52] Palau's domestic revenues include taxes, fees and charges, licenses, permits, and other direct revenues. In-kind foreign assistance, net investments—equal to the net change in the fair value of investments minus investment management fees—and other net financing are excluded due to market volatility associated with investment earnings and the prominent role in net financing of the compact-provided trust fund, which was designed to provide Palau with financing only until 2044.

[53] FAA's Airport Improvement Program grant to Palau represented more than $9 million of this assistance in 2006; it expired in 2007. The Airport Improvement Program's reauthorization for 2008-2011 is currently pending before Congress. It contains language that would continue Palau's eligibility for this program.

[54] IMF projected in 2006 the return required for the Palau trust fund to last until 2044 to be 10.4 percent. It assumed the disbursement is inflation adjusted while GAO's projection is based on the disbursement not being inflation adjusted.

[55] To calculate the compounded returns, we used the annual nominal returns published in 'BBOTSON Associates 2008 Yearbook. We rebalance the portfolio annually to maintain the asset allocation of 50 percent in U.S. large capital funds, 15 percent in U.S. small capital funds, and 35 percent in fixed income assets. See table 12 in appendix IV for the nominal and real returns of various time periods.

[56] Without market volatility, an 8.6 percent return rate would allow the trust fund to grow in perpetuity, as shown in figure 6.

[57] Compact section 215 states "the amounts stated in Sections 211(a), 211(b), 211(c) and 212(b) shall be adjusted for each fiscal year by the percent which equals two-thirds of the percentage change in the United States Gross National Product Implicit Price Deflator, or seven percent, whichever is less in any one year, using the beginning of fiscal year 1981 as the base." The annual distributions from the trust fund are not subject to section 215.

[58] We used the inflation rate projected by the Congressional Budget Office, which is lower than the historical inflation rate (from 1970 to 2007). A higher inflation rate will lead to further decline in value.

[59] See IMF, *Republic of Palau: 2005 Article IV Consultation – Staff Report* (Washington, D.C., March 2006). http://www.imf.org/external/pubs/cat/longres.cfm?sk=19023.0 (accessed May 27, 2008). The IMF's analysis of Palau's fiscal sustainability prospects recognizes that Palau will undergo a period of adjustment after compact direct assistance expires at the end of 2009 while pursuing economic reforms they suggest for implementation over a 10- to 15-year period.

[60] Absent market volatility, we estimate that the trust fund will likely grow in perpetuity if either the fund's compounded return rate or the asset classes' historical compounded return rate continues. Nonetheless, the IMF reports that Palau should decrease its dependence on the trust fund for annual financing. As a small island economy, Palau is vulnerable to external shocks, including damaging weather-related events, and trust fund assets could be reserved in order to enhance Palau's resiliency to such challenges.

[61] For example, a 2000 planning document prepared by the Japan International Cooperation Agency cites the need to reduce public sector employment by 40 percent between fiscal years 1999 and 2009, freeze public sector wages, privatize public sector enterprises, implement tax reform, and introduce vehicle-related taxes. Palau's Cost Reduction Plan of 2002 cites the need for government personnel restructuring, outsourcing services, and strengthening tax collection efforts.

[62] Although many noncompliant businesses may be smaller in size, the 30 largest taxpayers in Palau are estimated to provide 88 percent of tax revenues.

[63] This settlement of $1.25 million represents the outstanding principal of $645,000 plus 50 percent ($606,000) of the interest due of $1.2 million. The settlement excludes in full the $4 million of assessed penalties. Payments are to be made at a rate of not less than $10,000 per month, with the remaining balance accruing interest at a rate of 9 percent. Several Palau officials indicated

concern with the terms of this settlement because the former President of Palau served as a representative for the foreign-owned company.

[64] In addition to rising wage costs, government officials expressed concern about the financial soundness of the Civil Service Pension Fund. A 2005 actuarial valuation found that assets were sufficient to cover only 50 percent of liabilities. As such, the fund must draw on its investments to meet current obligations, which expanded in the late 1990s when state and college employees, who had not fully contributed to the plan, were added as beneficiaries.

[65] Economic research on the impact of road investments suggests a variety of possible benefits, including reduced transport costs, lowered input prices, increased access to markets, new migration opportunities, and improved information flow. The IMF finds infrastructure investment to be a statistically significant factor for increasing tourism expenditure in island economies. Palau officials reported that two hotels, a supermarket, and a port are planned for construction around the road. Despite potential benefits, Palau officials also expressed concern about environmental costs, including the introduction of invasive species from a reduction in the tree canopy, increased sediment run off, and watershed management problems.

[66] Tourist expenditure varies significantly by nationality. The ADB estimates the economic benefit from a U.S. tourist is about $900 per visit compared with about $150 per visit for a Taiwanese tourist. Many visitors from Taiwan travel on vouchers, where a large share of the money is paid to the travel agent rather than in country.

[67] Palau's tourism, agriculture, and fisheries sector are highly dependent on the environment and vulnerable to climate change. About 25 percent of Palau's landmass is less than 10 meters above sea level. El Niño events affect Palau significantly on a regular basis through decreased rainfall and increased sea water temperatures. Such events in 1997 and 1998 reportedly destroyed one-third of Palau's coral reefs, millions of its unique jellyfish, and most of its taro crops. See Palau's *First National Communication to the United National Framework Convention on Climate Change*, 2002.

[68] In 1997, a group of bank supervisors from advanced countries—the Basel Committee on Banking Supervision—issued the Core Principles for Effective Bank Supervision that provided best practices for financial regulation in developing countries. Since 1999, the IMF and World Bank have assessed member country compliance with the Basel principles. In 2002, the IMF assessed Palau's financial system as noncompliant on 16 of 25 Basel principles and reports improvements have not yet been made. The Financial Institutions Commission is working with the Palau Congress to revamp banking laws to be Basel compliant and is pursuing strengthened regulations.

[69] The Pacific Savings Bank, which held 20 percent of deposits in Palau, went into receivership in November 2006 due to inadequate capital and nonperforming insider loans. The ADB and Financial Institutions Commission attribute the bank failure to weak bank regulation. Potential costs to the government include the $1.4 million deposit of the national government, the $2.1 million deposit of the Palau Public Utilities Corporation, and the $1.5 million deposit of the Civil Service Pension Fund.

[70] Late payments by the government also have been a challenge for the Palau Public Utilities Corporation, which had a net loss of $6.6 million in 2005 and 2006. According to government officials, other factors contributing to this net loss include the cost of providing universal service under a fixed fee structure and an inability to raise rates quickly when oil prices rise.

[71] Unless otherwise noted, all years cited are fiscal years (Oct. 1-Sept. 30).

[72] At the time of this report, Palau's fiscal year 2007 single audit report had not been submitted and was not due for submission until June 30, 2008.

[73] The FAC operates on behalf of the Office of Management and Budget (OMB) and its primary purposes are to disseminate audit information to federal agencies and the public, support OMB oversight and assessment of federal award audit requirements, assist federal cognizant and oversight agencies in obtaining OMB Circular No. A-133 data and reporting packages, and, to help auditors and auditees minimize the reporting burden of complying with OMB Circular No. A-133 audit requirements.

[74] Compact of Free Association Act of 1985, Pub. L. No. 99-239, 99 Stat. 1770 (1986).

[75] Compact of Free Association with Micronesia and Marshall Island, Pub. L. No. 108-188, 117 Stat. 2720 (2003).

[76] For an in-depth discussion of the renegotiated FSM and RMI compacts, see GAO, *Compact of Free Association: An Assessment of the Amended Compacts and Related Agreements,* GAO-03-890T (Washington, D.C.: Jun. 18, 2003).

[77] Annual grant funding is reduced each year in order to encourage budgetary self-reliance and transition the countries from receiving annual U.S. grant funding to receiving annual trust fund earnings. Additional funds were provided related to the U.S. military use of Kwajalein Atoll.

[78] Palau government officials told us that there is no fixed schedule for disbursement and disbursement can happen throughout the year. In our simulation, we assume four equal quarterly disbursements at the end of each quarter each year.

[79] Compact section 215 states "the amounts stated in Sections 211(a), 211(b), 211(c) and 212(b) shall be adjusted for each fiscal year by the percent which equals two-thirds of the percentage change in the United States Gross National Product Implicit Price Deflator, or seven percent, whichever is less in any one year, using the beginning of Fiscal Year 1981 as the base." The annual distributions from the trust fund are not subject to section 215.

[80] The project is currently the subject of a construction contract dispute and the final U.S. cost of the project cannot be determined until the dispute is resolved.

[81] The compact road was designed and constructed to the same standards as noninterstate roads in the United States and included two 12-foot-wide asphalt paved lanes, designed to carry 400 to 2,500 vehicles per day, at speeds of up to 35 miles per hour, a pavement design life of 20 years, and a bridge design life of 100 years, providing they receive proper maintenance. The lower traffic volumes were used in the design of the road spur at the north end of the compact road and the highest volumes were used between the airport and Palau's capitol. The project also was designed and constructed to meet U.S. environmental laws and included the U.S. Fish and Wildlife Service, the National Marine Fisheries Service, and the U.S. Environmental Protection Agency as partners in the project.

[82] Maintenance requirements were set out in the subsidiary construction projects agreement known as *Agreement Regarding Construction Projects in Palau Concluded Pursuant to Section 212(a) of the Compact of Free Association.*

[83] USACE officials served as the project and program manager under an agreement with the Department of the Interior, in which USACE agreed to provide program and project management services, such as design management, contract procurement, and construction management.

[84] The term "double bituminous" was not defined in the compact, however, USACE interpreted the term to mean a two-layer application of asphalt and stone chips similar to what is typically identified as "chip and seal" and is found on many rural roads in the United States.

[85] Road specifications were set out in Annex A of the subsidiary construction projects agreement.

[86] Pub. L. No. 104-134, 110 Stat. 1321, 1321-174 (1996).

[87] Because the project was limited to 53 miles, the entire ring was not constructed by the United States and is currently being completed by Taiwan.

[88] Construction required cutting and filling several million cubic yards of earth, building seven bridges, and installing 20 box culverts and 372 culverts. The construction employed over 1,100 workers representing 10 different nationalities and required more than 500 pieces of heavy equipment at the peak of construction.

[89] Cut slope failures on the compact road are landslides that resulted directly from road construction activities that cut into hillsides.

[90] Expenses and budget data reported for the compact road are based on information received in interviews and have not been independently verified.

[91] Reported by USACE officials as of December 31, 2007.

[92] *Daewoo Eng'g and Constr. Co., LTD v. United States,* 73 Fed.Cl. 547 (2006) (notice of appeal filed on June 19, 2007).

[93] Examples of such emergencies are tropical storms and vehicle accidents.

[94] Crack sealing is a process of cleaning out cracks in the pavement and filling them with sealant to prevent water from getting under the pavement causing it to deteriorate.

[95] The Palau Bureau of Public Works includes several organizational divisions such as the Division of Facilities and Maintenance, Division of Road and Equipment, and Division of Utilities. The Division of Road and Equipment is further divided into branches including the Bridge and Road Maintenance Branch, which is responsible for maintaining the compact road.

[96] The decision to purchase a particular piece of equipment should include a justification process that considers all alternatives to accomplishing a task, including leasing, renting from other agencies or contractors, adapting an existing piece of equipment to perform the needed task, or contracting out the entire project. A piece of equipment may not be economically viable if not used sufficiently.

[97] See Pub. L. No. 110-229, Title VIII, Sec. 808, 122 Stat. 874 (May 8, 2008).

[98] See H.R. 2881, 110th Cong. (2007).

[99] 20 U.S.C. § 1091.

[100] While the formal title of the program is "Territories and Freely Associated States Education Grant," it is also known as the Freely Associated States Education Grant.

In: Palau and the Compact of Free Association …   ISBN: 978-1-62100-064-8
Editors: J. Berkin and P. D. O'Shaunessy   © 2012 Nova Science Publishers, Inc.

Chapter 7

PALAU PROFILE

United States Department of State

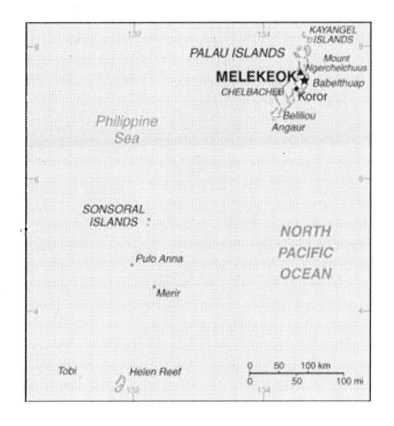

Flag of Palau

Official Name: Republic of Palau

PROFILE

Geography

Area: 458 sq. km. (about 190 sq. mi.) in eight main islands plus more than 250 islets.

Cities: *Capital*--Melekeok (pop. 391).

Terrain: Varies from mountainous main island to smaller, reef-rimmed coral islands.

Climate: Tropical.

People

Nationality: *Noun and adjective*--Palauan.

Population: Approximately 20,000 (non-Palauan population, approx. 6,000). *Age structure*--less than 15 years old, 5,150; 16-64 years old, 13,600; more than 65 years old, 1,130.

Population growth rate: 1.3%.

Ethnic groups: Palauans are Micronesian with Malayan and Melanesian elements.

Religion: Roman Catholic, Protestant, Modekngei (an indigenous Palauan religion).

Languages: English (official in all 16 states), Palauan.

Education: *Literacy*--95.2%.

Health: *Life expectancy*--male 68 yrs.; female 76 yrs. *Infant mortality rate*--16.2/1,000.

Work force: *Public sector*--33%; *private sector*--67%.

Government

Type: Constitutional republic in free association with United States.

Independence (from U.S.-administered UN trusteeship): October 1, 1994.

Constitution: January 1, 1981.

Branches: *Executive*--president (head of state and government), vice president, cabinet.

Legislative--bicameral parliament elected by popular vote. *Judicial*--Supreme Court, National Court, Court of Common Pleas, and the Land Court.

Economy

GDP (2009 est.): $178.4 million.

GDP per capita (2009 est.): $8,941.

National income (GDP + foreign assistance): estimated to be over $200 million.

National income per capita: estimated at $10,000.

GDP composition by sector: *Trade*--21%, *public administration*--20%, *construction*-15%, *hotels and restaurants*--10%, *finance and insurance*--8%, *transport and communication*--8%. Industry: *Types*--trade, government, construction, tourism.

Trade: *Exports* ($5.9 million, 2004)--fish, handicrafts. *Export markets*--U.S., Japan, and Taiwan. *Imports* ($129.5 million, 2008)--fuel and related minerals, machinery and transport equipment, beverages and tobacco, manufactured goods, and food and live animals. *Import sources*--U.S. (Guam), Japan, Singapore, Taiwan, and Korea.

External debt (2006): $38 million.

Currency: U.S. dollar.

GEOGRAPHY AND PEOPLE

The Republic of Palau consists of eight principal islands and more than 250 smaller ones lying roughly 500 miles southeast of the Philippines. The islands of Palau constitute part of the Caroline Islands chain. About 64% of Palauans live in Koror State's capital city, Koror. (Note: Government offices are located in a new National Capitol Building complex located at Ngerulmud, Melekeok State.)

HISTORY

Palau was initially settled more than 4,000 years ago, probably by migrants from what today is Indonesia. British traders became prominent visitors in the 18th century, followed by expanding Spanish influence in the 19th century. Following its defeat in the Spanish-American War, Spain sold Palau and most of the rest of the Caroline Islands to Germany in 1899. Control passed to Japan in 1914 and then to the United States under United Nations auspices in 1947 as part of the Trust Territory of the Pacific Islands.

Four of the Trust Territory districts formed a single federated Micronesian state in 1979, but this eventually dissolved as the individual districts--long culturally distinct--opted for more locally popular status. Palau approved a new constitution in 1981, subsequently signing a Compact of Free Association with the United States in 1982. After eight referenda and an amendment to the Palauan constitution, the Compact went into effect on October 1, 1994, marking Palau's emergence from trusteeship to independence.

GOVERNMENT

Palau is a democratic republic with directly elected executive and legislative branches. Presidential elections take place every 4 years, at the same time as the United States' presidential election, to select the president and the vice president, who now run as a team. The Palau National Congress (Olbiil era Kelulau) has two houses. The Senate has 13 members elected nationwide. The House of Delegates has 16 members, one each from Palau's 16 states. All of the legislators serve 4-year terms. Each state also elects its own governor and legislature.

The Council of Chiefs, comprising the highest traditional chiefs from each of the 16 states, is an advisory body to the president. The Council is consulted on matters concerning traditional laws and customs.

The judicial system consists of the Supreme Court--with trial and appellate divisions--the Court of Common Pleas, and the Land Court. (Palau's constitution has a provision for an additional National Court, but this is not currently active.)

In November 2008 Palauans elected a new president and vice president: Johnson Toribiong and Kerai Mariur. They took office on January 15, 2009. The same elections brought sweeping change to the legislature and passed more than 20 amendments to the constitution.

Principal Government Officials

Head of State and Government--President Johnson Toribiong
Vice President--Kerai Mariur
Ambassador to the U.S.--Hersey Kyota
Ambassador to the UN--Stuart Beck

Palau maintains an embassy at 1700 Pennsylvania Avenue, Suite 400, Washington, DC 20006 (tel: 202-452-6814, fax: 202-452-6281). The Republic of Palau's Mission to the United Nations is located at 866 United Nations Plaza, Suite 575, New York, New York 10017 (tel: 212-813-0310, fax: 212-813-0317). Palau also has embassies in Japan, Philippines, and Taiwan.

POLITICAL CONDITIONS

The government is stable, with national elections held every 4 years in the executive branch and Congress. Elections are free and fair, and candidates rely heavily on media campaigns, town meetings, and rallies. There are no political parties, and candidates run on their own platforms.

Legislation making Palau an "offshore" financial center was passed by the Senate in 1998. In 2001 Palau passed its first bank regulation and anti-money laundering laws.

ECONOMY

Palau's per capita GDP of $8,941 makes it one of the wealthier Pacific Island states. Nominal GDP increased by an annual average of nearly 14% from 1983 to 1990, and by an annual rate of over 10% from 1991 to 1997. Growth turned sharply negative in 1998 and 1999 as a result of the Asian financial crisis, but a gradual rebound followed, and the economy grew by 5.6% in 2007.

Tourism (and its attendant infrastructure changes) is Palau's main industry. Its major draws are its diverse and pristine marine environment, and its above-water tropical island beauty. The number of visitors--34% from Japan, 26% from Taiwan, 18% from Korea, and 11% from the U.S.--was 85,593 in 2010, a 10% increase from 2009. Continental Airlines has direct flights to Palau from Guam and the Philippines. Delta Airlines has weekly non-stop flights from Narita, Japan to Palau. Japan Airlines runs chartered flights from Tokyo, and Korean Airlines does the same from Seoul on a seasonal basis.

Palauan tourism and environmental authorities would like to adjust the industry, simultaneously decreasing tourist volume and increasing income by attracting more high-dollar tourists.

The service sector dominates the Palauan economy, contributing more than 50% of GDP and employing more than half of the work force. The government alone employs about 30% of workers and accounts for 20% of the GDP.

Construction is an important industrial activity, contributing over 15% of GDP. Several large infrastructure projects, roads, and hotels have boosted this sector's recent contribution to GDP.

Agriculture is mainly on a subsistence level, the principal crops being coconuts, taro, and bananas. Fishing is a potential source of revenue, but the islands' tuna output dropped by over one-third during the 1990s. Fishing industry revenues are mostly from license fees from fishing vessels.

One of the government's main responsibilities is administering external assistance, and the main economic challenge confronting Palau is to ensure the long-term viability of its economy by reducing its reliance on foreign assistance.

Under the terms of the Compact of Free Association with the United States, Palau received more than $800 million in direct assistance over 15 years and exercised its prerogative to participate in a wide range of federal programs. In early September 2010, the United States and Palau concluded a 15-year comprehensive review of the Compact. A wide range of federal programs will continue for the next 15 years. By the end of 2010, the value of a trust fund set up under the Compact was approximately $160 million.

FOREIGN RELATIONS

Palau gained its independence October 1, 1994 with the entry into force of the Compact of Free Association with the United States. Palau was the last component of the Trust Territory of the Pacific Islands to gain its independence. Under the Compact, the U.S. remains responsible for Palau's defense for 50 years. The two countries concluded a comprehensive review of the Compact in 2010.

Palau is a sovereign nation and conducts its own foreign relations. Since independence, Palau has established diplomatic relations with a number of nations, including many of its Pacific neighbors, and is one of two dozen or so nations that have diplomatic relations with Taiwan. Palau was admitted to the United Nations on December 15, 1994, and has since joined a number of other international organizations. Palau is a dependable supporter of U.S. positions in the UN.

CHAPTER SOURCES

The following chapters have been previously published:

Chapter 1 – This is an edited, reformatted and augmented version of a United States Government Accountability Office publication, Report GAO-11-559T, dated June 16, 2011.

Chapter 2 – These remarks were delivered as testimony given on June 16, 2011. H. E. Johnson Toribiong, President of the Freely Associated State of Palau, Before the Senate Committee on Energy and Natural Resources.

Chapter 3 – These remarks were delivered as testimony given on June 16, 2011. Frankie Reed, Deputy Assistant Secretary of State, Bureau of East Asian and Pacific Affairs, United States Department of State, Before the Senate Committee on Energy and Natural Resources.

Chapter 4 – These remarks were delivered as testimony given on June 16, 2011. Anthony M. Babauta, Assistant Secretary of the Interior-Insular Areas, Department of the Interior, Before the Senate Committee on Energy and Natural Resources.

Chapter 5 – These remarks were delivered as testimony given on June 16, 2011. Robert Scher, Deputy Assistant Secretary of Defense, South and Southeast Asia, Before the Senate Committee on Energy and Natural Resources.

Chapter 6 – This is an edited, reformatted and augmented version of a United States Government Accountability Office publication, Report GAO-08-732, dated June 2008.

Chapter 7 - This is an edited, reformatted and augmented version of a United States Department of State publication, dated May 2011.

INDEX

#

9/11, 34, 47

A

abuse, 135
access, 35, 41, 45, 46, 47, 49, 57, 61, 80, 83, 85, 92, 94, 95, 109
accountability, viii, 51, 52, 55, 56, 64, 74, 76, 77, 78, 89, 90, 92, 93, 133
accounting, 3, 8, 15, 52, 56, 74, 76, 89, 134, 135
adjustment, 67, 68, 91, 99, 133, 136
administrators, 119
adult education, 70
advancement, vii, viii, 1, 3, 51, 54, 61, 88
advancements, 44
advisory body, 144
affirmative action, 83, 89
Afghanistan, 28, 34, 35, 47
age, 57, 72, 86
agencies, vii, viii, 1, 3, 6, 8, 9, 11, 13, 14, 20, 27, 37, 51, 53, 55, 56, 57, 62, 63, 64, 65, 66, 69, 70, 71, 72, 75, 77, 83, 89, 90, 98, 114, 117, 118, 131, 133, 135, 137, 139
agriculture, 137
AIDS, 18, 122
Air Force, 48
airports, 90, 114
Albania, 27
alters, 20
American Samoa, 34, 118

ancestors, 24
annual rate, 145
appropriations, 8, 10, 11, 14, 15, 21, 26, 44, 83, 95, 132
aquaculture, 87
armed forces, 5, 6
Asia, 34, 37, 45, 46, 47, 49, 87
Asia-Pacific region, 45, 46, 47, 49
assessment, 77, 137
assets, 48, 61, 80, 95, 105, 115, 135, 136, 137
audit, 2, 4, 18, 20, 36, 52, 54, 55, 56, 60, 62, 63, 72, 74, 75, 76, 78, 80, 89, 90, 91, 92, 97, 98, 114, 124, 132, 133, 134, 135, 137
audits, 5, 7, 27, 64, 66, 71, 76, 85, 89, 91, 97, 132, 133, 134, 135
authorities, 7, 86, 107, 113, 146
authority, 4, 5, 6, 8, 10, 14, 20, 21, 25, 32, 47, 58, 63, 72, 85, 93, 132
aviation services, 6, 10, 43, 57, 62, 68, 70, 79, 83, 134
awareness, 48

B

balanced budget, 36
bank failure, 137
banking, 87, 88, 137
banking industry, 87
bankruptcy, 88
base, 25, 27, 40, 41, 68, 92, 134, 136, 138
basing rights, 25
benchmarks, 119
beneficiaries, 137
benefits, 21, 88, 105, 137

beverages, 143
bilateral relationship, 31, 37, 41
blood, 32, 33, 37
border security, 27
business environment, 53, 57, 79, 86, 87
businesses, 85, 86, 87, 136

C

campaigns, 145
candidates, 145
capacity building, 35, 120
capital account, 67, 68
capital expenditure, 85
capital projects, 42
career development, 72
Caroline Islands, viii, 59, 143, 144
cash, 69, 76
catalyst, 29
· CDC, 18
Chairman Bingaman, 3, 15, 23, 31, 39
challenges, 31, 52, 58, 75, 89, 91, 92, 105,
    107, 109, 110, 136
• child development, 116
childhood, 72
children, 34, 35, 72, 94, 116, 117
China, 27, 28, 33, 46, 48
citizens, 5, 6, 20, 34, 35, 62, 94, 132
civil service, 21
classes, 82, 84, 100, 102, 105, 136
cleaning, 113, 139
climate, 53, 79, 137
climate change, 137
closure, 115
coal, 44
Coast Guard, 35, 48
collateral, 87
commercial, 53, 79, 87, 88, 134
Commonwealth of the Northern Mariana
    Islands, 4, 34, 47, 58
communication, 46, 143
community, 40, 48, 52, 72, 116, 118, 121
community relations, 72, 121
community service, 48

Compact Road, vii, 1, 2, 5, 6, 7, 9, 21, 42, 70,
    105, 106, 107, 108, 109, 111
Compact with Palau, 25, 31, 36, 45, 47
compaction, 109
compliance, 52, 56, 64, 74, 75, 76, 77, 85, 87,
    89, 91, 132, 133, 135, 137
composition, 10, 143
computer, 34
conference, 6, 63
conflict, 25
conformity, 134
congress, 7, 8, 10, 20, 23, 26, 28, 29, 37, 63,
    66, 83, 89, 113, 115, 132, 134, 136, 137,
    144, 145
congressional budget, 24
Congressional Budget Office, 100, 136
congressional rules, 23
consent, 6, 61
conservation, 35
consolidation, 2, 9, 10, 17, 42
constitution, 143
construction, vii, 1, 52, 54, 56, 65, 68, 70, 72,
    88, 92, 105, 109, 110, 111, 121, 137, 138,
    143
continental, 145
Continental Airlines, 145
controversial, 33
cooperation, 48
coordination, 48, 135
coral reefs, 137
correlation, 102
cost, 6, 26, 43, 53, 57, 65, 66, 69, 72, 83, 90,
    96, 97, 107, 110, 111, 113, 114, 116, 117,
    132, 133, 134, 137, 138
cost-benefit analysis, 111
cracks, 112, 139
creditors, 10, 42
crops, 137, 146
Cuba, 27, 33
current account, 5, 62, 67, 132
curriculum, 70, 119
curriculum development, 71, 119
customers, 120
Customs and Border Protection, 95
cyclones, 6, 43, 69

D

Daewoo, 92, 138
danger, 5, 29
data collection, 91
database, 134
debt service, 97
debts, 10
deficiencies, 20, 109, 135
Delta, 145
democracy, 33, 36, 40
denial, 5, 6, 45
Department of Agriculture, 37, 54, 119, 124
Department of Commerce, 132
Department of Defense, v, 28, 37, 45, 53, 120
Department of Education, 53, 70, 115, 117, 118
Department of Health and Human Services, 19, 53, 116, 117
Department of Homeland Security, 94
Department of Labor, 72, 88
Department of the Interior (DOI), v, viii, 4, 24, 36, 37, 39, 40, 44, 51, 53, 53, 55, 58, 89, 125, 126, 138
Department of Transportation (DOT), 53, 55, 56, 72, 90, 114, 121
Departments of Agriculture, 55
deposits, 137
depth, 138
designers, 108
destiny, 40
destruction, 109
detainees, 27, 35, 47
developing countries, 137
deviation, 102
disaster, 34, 72
disaster relief, 34, 72
disbursement, 2, 4, 68, 84, 91, 99, 100, 136, 138
discretionary federal programs, vii, 1, 3, 6, 7, 8, 9, 11, 14, 15, 20, 53, 54, 56, 57, 62, 63, 65, 66, 73, 79, 83, 88, 97, 98, 114, 132, 133
distribution, 12, 54, 61, 82, 91, 99, 102, 132, 134
diversity, 114

donations, 69, 117
donors, 13, 61, 132
draft, 58
drainage, 113
drawing, 43

E

earnings, 57, 60, 68, 80, 86, 95, 98, 100, 136, 138
East Asia, v, 31
economic advancement, vii, viii, 1, 3, 51, 54, 61, 88
economic assistance, vii, viii, 1, 2, 3, 4, 8, 9, 10, 17, 36, 42, 43, 51, 54, 92, 93
economic development, 21, 35, 42, 54, 56, 64, 70, 77, 91, 105, 106, 110, 111, 133
economic growth, 40, 41
economic power, 28
economic reform, 41, 43, 136
education, vii, 1, 3, 5, 9, 10, 35, 40, 42, 43, 48, 52, 62, 67, 68, 70, 72, 88, 93, 94, 95, 114, 116, 117, 118
educational services, 119
election, 144
electricity, 68
elementary school, 117
embassy, 145
emergency, 72, 113, 115
emergency repairs, 72
employees, 43, 78, 113, 135, 137
employment, 86, 87, 91, 136
energy, 5, 36, 40, 62, 68
enforcement, 67, 72
engineering, 48, 109
enrollment, 72, 116
environment, 36, 46, 79, 93, 109, 110, 121, 137
environmental conditions, 105
Environmental Protection Agency, 138
environmental resources, 87
equipment, 69, 72, 76, 92, 109, 111, 113, 115, 134, 138, 139, 143
equities, 34, 46, 47
European Union, 58

evidence, 4, 49, 56, 92
executive branch, 23, 29, 59, 66, 145
Executive Order, 33, 133
expenditures, 7, 21, 41, 53, 57, 60, 61, 65, 66, 69, 71, 79, 85, 86, 90, 95, 96, 97, 114, 132, 134, 135
expertise, 52, 56, 74, 76, 89
exploitation, 48, 87
external shocks, 136

F

FAA, 6, 7, 53, 55, 58, 66, 69, 70, 72, 90, 93, 114, 115, 121, 134, 136
faith, 20, 78, 133
families, 73, 116
family planning, 72
federal assistance, 89
federal funds, viii, 51, 55, 64, 78, 89, 90
Federal Highway Administration, 114
Federated States of Micronesia (FSM), 45, 55, 58, 92, 98
fencing, 72, 115
fiber, 120
financial, viii, 9, 21, 36, 37, 39, 40, 42, 43, 51, 52, 53, 55, 56, 57, 58, 64, 71, 74, 75, 76, 78, 79, 87, 88, 89, 91, 115, 132, 133, 134, 135, 137, 145
financial condition, 135
financial crisis, 37, 145
financial data, 133, 134
financial markets, 87
financial oversight, 57
financial regulation, 87, 88, 137
financial soundness, 137
financial system, 53, 79, 87, 137
fire fighting, 72
fiscal year 2009, viii, 51
fish, 86, 143
Fish and Wildlife Service, 138
fisheries, 72, 137
fishing, 46, 48, 87, 146
flank, 37
flight, 6, 44, 70, 134
flights, 145

food, 143
force, vii, viii, 1, 3, 4, 5, 6, 20, 32, 51, 54, 58, 63, 69, 131, 142, 146
foreign affairs, 5, 62
foreign aid, 4, 61
foreign assistance, 60, 98, 132, 136, 143, 146
foreign banks, 87
foreign direct investment, 87
foreign investment, 41, 53, 57, 79, 87
foreign policy, 32
formal language, 32
fraud, 135
free association, 25, 98, 143
freedom, 24, 33
friendship, 27, 33
funding, 13, 15, 26, 36, 40, 63, 64, 66, 68, 70, 72, 78, 83, 89, 93, 98, 105, 107, 110, 111, 112, 113, 115, 116, 117, 121, 124, 125, 132, 133, 138
funds, viii, 4, 5, 9, 14, 18, 20, 21, 32, 51, 52, 54, 57, 62, 64, 65, 68, 72, 74, 77, 78, 89, 93, 98, 105, 111, 114, 115, 116, 117, 119, 120, 132, 136, 138

G

GAO, vii, viii, 1, 2, 3, 4, 6, 7, 8, 12, 13, 14, 16, 17, 19, 20, 21, 41, 51, 52, 59, 60, 63, 66, 67, 69, 71, 73, 80, 81, 82, 97, 98, 100, 101, 102, 104, 105, 106, 108, 112, 136, 138
GDP per capita, 20, 61, 98, 143
geography, 37
Germany, viii, 144
global security, 49
goods and services, 60
governance, 32
government budget, 89, 90, 91
government expenditure, 61
government revenues, vii, 1, 4, 15, 21, 53, 57, 83
government spending, 85
governments, viii, 3, 4, 8, 9, 20, 31, 32, 43, 51, 54, 55, 57, 58, 61, 64, 68, 77, 88, 91, 121, 133, 135
governor, 59, 144

grant programs, 43, 72, 133
grants, 2, 5, 9, 10, 11, 13, 17, 40, 42, 52, 61, 62, 64, 66, 67, 70, 72, 76, 93, 95, 114, 115, 116, 117, 132, 133, 134, 135
grass, 111, 112, 113
gravity, 37
greed, 58
gross domestic product (GDP), 4, 20, 21, 53, 60, 61, 85, 87, 96, 97, 98, 132, 143, 145, 146
growth, 40, 41, 53, 57, 79, 80, 86, 87, 97, 142
growth rate, 79, 80, 97, 142
Guantanamo, 27, 35, 47
guidance, 92, 111, 113
guidelines, 116

H

Hawaii, 34, 47, 136
health, vii, 1, 3, 5, 9, 10, 40, 42, 43, 48, 52, 62, 67, 68, 70, 72, 88, 93, 94, 95, 114, 116, 118
Health and Human Services (HHS), 8, 18, 19, 37, 44, 53, 55, 56, 63, 72, 90, 116, 121, 122
health care, 40, 52, 118
health status, 118
high school, 117
higher education, 134
hiring, 76
history, 29
HIV, 18, 19, 122
host, 121
hotel, 86
hotels, 137, 143, 146
house, 26, 36, 54, 144
House of Representatives, 54
housing, 73
human, 33, 36
human right, 33, 36

I

ideals, 27
identification, 95

identity, 33, 34, 94
immigration, 5, 62, 92, 94
immunization, 72
improvements, 9, 40, 52, 55, 56, 58, 68, 74, 76, 90, 115, 137
income, 10, 20, 21, 57, 61, 65, 85, 86, 96, 99, 100, 102, 105, 116, 136, 143, 146
income tax, 21
increased access, 137
increased competition, 120
independence, 25, 32, 58, 143, 144, 146
individual students, 115
individuals, 47, 73, 92, 95
Individuals with Disabilities Education Act, 117
Indonesia, viii, 25, 144
industries, 87
industry, 48, 111, 145, 146
inflation, 14, 15, 27, 53, 57, 68, 79, 80, 84, 90, 91, 97, 99, 100, 133, 136
infrastructure, vii, 1, 2, 3, 9, 21, 26, 33, 42, 48, 55, 70, 72, 73, 88, 90, 93, 94, 114, 115, 120, 132, 137, 145, 146
in-kind services, 70
institutions, 11, 21
instructional materials, 119
internal controls, 56, 76, 89, 132, 135
International Monetary Fund (IMF), 20, 21, 53, 55, 85, 86, 87, 90, 91, 100, 136, 137
intervention, 115
investment, 2, 4, 36, 52, 54, 57, 60, 68, 78, 84, 86, 87, 95, 97, 100, 102, 115, 132, 136, 137
investment incentive, 57
investments, 3, 9, 42, 95, 96, 97, 111, 136, 137
investors, 87
Iraq, 28, 35, 47
IRC, 124
islands, 4, 23, 24, 25, 27, 32, 41, 49, 58, 59, 118, 142, 143, 146
Israel, 27, 33
issues, 27, 33, 41, 64, 65, 75, 78, 92, 135

J

Japan, viii, 4, 24, 34, 35, 48, 58, 61, 77, 136, 143, 144, 145
job training, 72
judicial branch, 59, 66
jurisdiction, 24, 44
justification, 7, 66, 67, 125, 139

K

kindergarten, 116
Korea, 143, 145

L

labor force, 20, 61
labor market, 87
law enforcement, 35, 48
laws, 25, 44, 52, 74, 76, 88, 92, 119, 132, 135, 137, 138, 144, 145
laws and regulations, 52, 74, 132
lawyers, 100
lead, 24, 29, 53, 84, 136
leadership, 23, 34, 36, 46
Lebanon, 28
legislation, 9, 10, 11, 21, 23, 24, 26, 31, 32, 33, 34, 35, 36, 37, 44, 46, 49, 63, 86, 94, 95, 107, 113, 114, 115, 116, 117, 118, 119, 120, 132, 134
legislative proposals, 44
license fee, 87, 146
liquidity, 87
litigation, 92
loans, 7, 66, 70, 71, 73, 119, 134, 137
local government, 98
LTD, 138
lying, 143

M

machinery, 143
maintenance tasks, 111, 113

majority, 26, 28, 56, 59, 70, 74, 77
man, 48, 111
management, 9, 21, 43, 52, 58, 64, 76, 78, 89, 93, 95, 97, 110, 114, 115, 132, 133, 136, 137, 138
management committee, 93
mandatory retirement, 119
man-made disasters, 111
manpower, 109, 113
manufactured goods, 143
Marine Corps, 35
marine environment, 145
maritime security, 48
Marshall Islands, 4, 11, 34, 45, 47, 48, 54, 55, 58, 92, 98
materials, 109, 121
media, 145
medical, 48, 68, 72, 116, 121
methodology, 56, 84, 100
migrants, viii, 144
migration, 137
military, 5, 6, 25, 28, 34, 35, 37, 40, 46, 47, 48, 63, 87, 92, 94, 120, 138
minimum wage, 88
Ministry of Education, 117, 118, 119
mission, 132
missions, 34, 48
modernization, 85
modifications, viii, 51, 55, 110
moisture, 109
moisture content, 109
money laundering, 145
mortality, 142
mortality rate, 142
Moses, 34
Muslims, 27

N

national interests, 33
national security, 31, 39, 46, 47, 49, 61
nationality, 137
natural disaster, 72
negotiating, 107
net investment, 80, 95, 136

No Child Left Behind, 118
nutrition, 116

O

Office of Management and Budget, 53, 133,
    137
Office of the Inspector General, 53, 64, 89
officials, viii, 21, 23, 26, 28, 29, 35, 48, 51,
    52, 55, 57, 69, 70, 71, 72, 76, 77, 78, 83,
    85, 86, 87, 88, 89, 90, 91, 92, 93, 94, 105,
    107, 109, 110, 111, 112, 113, 115, 117,
    118, 119, 120, 121, 134, 135, 136, 137, 138
oil, 44, 137
operating costs, 71
operations, 2, 5, 6, 9, 10, 34, 40, 43, 48, 52,
    56, 58, 62, 65, 67, 68, 69, 88, 110, 114,
    115, 132
opportunities, 21, 86, 111, 137
outreach, 121, 134
outreach programs, 134
outsourcing, 113, 136
oversight, viii, 51, 52, 57, 64, 74, 77, 78, 91,
    137
ownership, 87

P

Pacific, v, viii, 4, 21, 24, 25, 31, 32, 33, 34,
    35, 36, 37, 39, 40, 41, 45, 46, 47, 48, 49,
    54, 58, 59, 85, 87, 117, 132, 137, 144, 145,
    146
Palau government, vii, viii, 1, 3, 4, 8, 9, 10,
    13, 20, 21, 40, 42, 51, 54, 57, 61, 64, 65,
    72, 75, 77, 87, 88, 89, 90, 91, 92, 115, 133,
    135, 138
Palau government revenues, vii, 1, 4, 21
participants, 116, 134
peace, 24, 28, 34
penalties, 85, 136
Philippines, 4, 20, 25, 32, 59, 61, 88, 143, 145
policy, 24, 86
political parties, 145
popular vote, 143

population, 4, 14, 34, 59, 88, 97, 121, 142
population growth, 14
port of entry, 94
portfolio, 84, 99, 105, 136
postal service, 6, 11, 27, 43, 69, 134
potential benefits, 137
preparation, iv, 94
president, v, 10, 23, 31, 33, 35, 36, 44, 137,
    143, 144, 145
primacy, 34
principles, 33, 40, 134, 137
probability, 11, 12, 21, 82, 84, 100
problem-solving, 100
project, 2, 3, 9, 14, 15, 17, 55, 70, 85, 89, 100,
    105, 107, 109, 110, 111, 121, 138, 139
protection, 88
protectorate, 37, 40
public administration, 143
public broadcasting, 68
public education, 117
public health, 88, 118
Public Health Service Act, 118
public safety, 9, 10, 42, 43
public schools, 73
public sector, 4, 9, 20, 41, 57, 61, 86, 98, 113,
    136

Q

qualifications, 119

R

rainfall, 137
rate of return, 84
raw materials, 121
reading, 119
real property, 76
real terms, 40
recognition, 120
recommendations, 9, 20, 52, 64, 78
reconstruction, 111
reform, 21, 37, 42, 53, 57, 79, 84, 86, 119
reforms, 9, 21, 27, 41, 42, 43, 53, 57, 79, 85

regulations, 57, 76, 87, 133, 135, 137
rehabilitation, 68
reliability, 52, 56, 74, 75, 89, 91, 135
religion, 142
remittances, 20, 61, 98
repair, 36, 73, 111, 113
Republic of Palau, v, vii, viii, 1, 2, 3, 6, 8, 14, 16, 17, 19, 20, 21, 31, 39, 41, 51, 54, 58, 128, 132, 133, 136, 142, 143, 145
Republic of the Marshall Islands (RMI), 45, 55, 58, 92, 98
requirements, 20, 21, 24, 26, 52, 56, 63, 64, 74, 76, 77, 78, 87, 89, 91, 93, 95, 109, 133, 135, 137, 138
resettlement, 47
resolution, 6, 63, 133
resources, 41, 42, 48, 52, 56, 74, 78, 89, 113, 114
response, 24, 26, 27
restaurants, 143
restructuring, 136
revenue, 3, 11, 13, 14, 21, 27, 40, 41, 42, 60, 69, 80, 85, 95, 96, 97, 98, 120, 146
rights, 5, 6, 25, 27, 28, 49, 62, 63
risk, 52, 56, 74, 76, 89, 135
risks, 85
rotations, 72, 121
routes, 115
rules, 23, 26, 94, 135
rural areas, 119
Rural Utilities Service, 119
Russia, 46

S

SACE, 55, 90
safety, 72, 112, 115
savings, 44
scholarship, 67
school, 32, 58, 68, 116, 117, 119, 121, 134
school improvement, 119
scope, 9, 56, 105, 107, 110
sea level, 137
Secretary of Defense, v, 35, 45
securities, 78
security, 3, 5, 6, 7, 23, 24, 28, 32, 33, 34, 35, 36, 37, 45, 46, 47, 48, 49, 54, 61, 63, 72, 115, 133, 135
sediment, 137
self-sufficiency, vii, viii, 1, 3, 33, 36, 51, 52, 54, 55, 57, 61, 67, 68, 79, 83, 84, 86, 88, 89, 91, 106, 134
senate, 4, 20, 21, 36, 54, 144, 145
Senator Murkowski, 23, 31
service provider, 134
services, vii, 1, 3, 5, 6, 7, 8, 9, 10, 13, 14, 20, 21, 26, 27, 28, 37, 40, 41, 43, 44, 52, 53, 54, 55, 56, 57, 60, 62, 63, 65, 66, 67, 68, 69, 70, 79, 80, 83, 85, 88, 90, 93, 96, 97, 98, 111, 113, 116, 117, 118, 120, 126, 131, 134, 136, 138
siblings, 28, 34
signs, 112
simulation, 91, 99, 100, 102, 138
Singapore, 143
skilled workers, 57
Social Security, 20, 95, 100, 132
solution, 25
South Korea, 34
Southeast Asia, v, 45, 46
sovereign nation, 25, 40, 58, 146
sovereignty, 3, 7, 24, 40, 58
Spain, viii, 144
Spanish-American War, viii, 144
special education, 11, 117
species, 137
specifications, 6, 70, 106, 138
spending, 4, 20, 26, 27, 78, 85
stability, 41
staff members, 23
stakeholders, 108, 109
standard deviation, 102
state, 10, 25, 27, 28, 34, 36, 40, 68, 98, 111, 114, 121, 137, 143, 144
states, 10, 23, 25, 27, 28, 33, 44, 46, 49, 59, 63, 66, 68, 78, 98, 109, 119, 120, 121, 133, 134, 136, 138, 142, 144, 145
statistics, 61, 88, 98, 116
storage, 111
strategic position, 47

structure, 57, 137, 142
subsidy, 27
subsistence, 24, 146
supervision, 87, 110
supervisors, 137
Supreme Court, 143, 144
surface treatment, 107
surveillance, 48, 67, 72
sustainability, 4, 85, 136
sustainable growth, 86

T

Taiwan, 4, 48, 58, 61, 137, 138, 143, 145, 146
target, 58, 89
tax collection, 136
tax policy, 85, 86
tax reform, 9, 43, 86, 136
tax system, 85
taxation, 21
taxes, 13, 80, 85, 86, 97, 111, 136
taxpayers, 85, 136
teacher training, 70, 119
teachers, 117, 119
teaching strategies, 119
teams, 48, 72, 120
technical assistance, 6, 15, 44, 58, 69, 70, 72,
    78, 89, 111, 131, 134
technical change, 107
technical comments, 58
techniques, 110
technology, 119
telecommunications, 27, 70, 72, 120
telephone, 119
territory, 24, 25, 58, 59
terrorism, 34, 132
theft, 76
time periods, 99, 136
Title I, 20, 32, 45
Title V, 134, 139
tobacco, 143
total revenue, 61
tourism, 4, 61, 86, 132, 137, 143, 146
trade, 143
trainees, 121

training, 6, 34, 44, 48, 69, 70, 72, 110, 114,
    119, 121, 134
transactions, 135
transport, 137, 143
transport costs, 137
transportation, 36, 69
treatment, 88
trial, 12, 82, 100, 102, 144
tropical storms, 139
trust fund, vii, 1, 2, 3, 4, 5, 7, 9, 10, 11, 12, 14,
    21, 25, 33, 36, 37, 40, 41, 42, 43, 52, 53,
    54, 55, 57, 60, 61, 62, 64, 67, 68, 78, 79,
    80, 81, 82, 83, 84, 91, 93, 95, 96, 97, 98,
    99, 100, 102, 103, 105, 132, 134, 136, 138,
    146
Trust Territory of the Pacific Islands, viii, 4,
    32, 58, 132, 144, 146
tutoring, 121

U

U.N. Security Council, 24
U.S. Army Corps of Engineers, 54, 55, 90
U.S. assistance, vii, viii, 1, 3, 4, 5, 7, 8, 9, 10,
    14, 15, 40, 51, 52, 55, 57, 63, 65, 70, 78,
    79, 83, 88, 89, 90, 91, 96, 97, 98, 131, 134
U.S. Treasury, 100, 101, 102
uniform, 34, 133
united, v, vi, vii, viii, 1, 2, 3, 4, 5, 6, 8, 9, 10,
    14, 20, 21, 23, 24, 25, 26, 27, 28, 29, 32,
    33, 34, 35, 36, 37, 39, 40, 41, 42, 43, 45,
    46, 47, 48, 49, 51, 54, 55, 58, 61, 62, 63,
    65, 68, 69, 70, 73, 78, 88, 89, 92, 93, 94,
    98, 99, 106, 107, 109, 110, 113, 114, 116,
    119, 120, 132, 133, 134, 136, 137, 138,
    143, 144, 145, 146
United Nations (UN), viii, 4, 24, 25, 27, 32,
    40, 58, 132, 143, 144, 145, 146
United Nations Trust Territory of the Pacific
    Islands, 24, 40
United States, v, vi, vii, viii, 1, 2, 3, 4, 5, 6, 8,
    9, 10, 14, 20, 21, 23, 24, 25, 26, 27, 28, 29,
    32, 33, 34, 35, 36, 37, 39, 40, 41, 42, 43,
    45, 46, 47, 48, 49, 51, 54, 55, 58, 61, 62,
    63, 65, 68, 69, 70, 73, 78, 88, 89, 92, 93,

94, 98, 99, 106, 107, 109, 110, 113, 114,
  116, 119, 120, 132, 133, 134, 136, 138,
  143, 144, 146
United States law, 23, 25, 29
updating, 76
urban, 4, 59
USDA, 54, 55, 58, 72, 73, 90, 119, 124

V

valuation, 137
variables, 100
vehicles, 115, 138
vessels, 48, 146
veto, 94
Vice President, 145
Vietnam, 28
vision, 36
volatility, 11, 53, 57, 60, 79, 84, 85, 92, 95,
  100, 136
volunteers, 35
vote, 33
vouchers, 137

W

wage level, 86, 98
wages, 85, 136
war, 28, 40, 48
Washington, 20, 73, 136, 138, 145
waste, 135
water, 5, 36, 47, 68, 108, 109, 137, 139, 145
watershed, 137
weakness, 76, 135
WIA, 19
Wisconsin, 114
withdrawal, 12, 13, 21, 36, 43, 60, 80, 84, 85,
  100
workers, 20, 61, 88, 111, 113, 132, 138, 146
workforce, 9
Workforce Investment Act, 72, 123
workload, 112
World Bank, 137
world community, 40
World War I, 4, 24, 32, 34, 36, 40, 48, 58, 109

Y

yield, 11, 43